SO YOU GOT THE JOB!

WTF IS NEXT?

PROVEN STEPS TO SUCCEED IN ANY NEW JOB

GREG WEISS

"So You Got The Job! WTF Is Next" by Greg Weiss

Published by Ingram Spark

www.wtfisnext.wtf

© 2019 Global Personal Consulting Pty Limited ACN 52 991 497 240

For information about special discounts available for bulk purchases, sales promotions, fund-raising and educational needs, contact Global Personal Consulting Pty Limited or **sales@wtfisnext.wtf**

ISBN: 978-0-6484607-1-8

For my two wonderful and talented, millennial-era, adult children, Sam and Mimi, who along with their friends and cousins, have their careers ahead of them.

Make a difference in your own ways.
The world needs you.

Illustrations by Sacha Rena

sacharena.com

WORDS OF THANKS FROM GREG WEISS

Thank you for picking up a copy of this book.

I have been encouraged by many people over the years to write a book. Now that it has been done, I can admit that it feels much like becoming a new parent. Excited, delighted, relieved, curious, unsure...

Your support means a lot to me.

If you find this book helpful, here are the best ways to help me spread the word:

Please leave a review of the book on Amazon or wherever you bought this book. Posting a review is easy and doesn't take much time. Detailed reviews help new readers discover how they too can benefit from this book.

Donate a copy to your local public library or institution of higher education or learning.

Give it as a gift to anyone you know who is about to start a new job.

If you have any questions, or you'd like to share how this book helped you, you can reach me via **gregw@wtfisnext.wtf**

Thanks :)

Greg Weiss

ACKNOWLEDGEMENT AND THANKS

I am particularly proud to feature the art of a very talented 15 year old throughout this book. I hope Sacha, that you continue to doodle and draw your way to success. You can find Sacha's work via sacharena.com

To my darling wife, Debbi. Thanks for your love, support, belief and encouragement. You've known about my dream to write a book for the past 30 years. Now that it's done, I promise it won't take the next 30 to get the next one out!

To my children Sam and Mimi, I am so proud of who you are - always have been - always will be. But the most important thing in life is that you are proud of the person you are and the life you make for yourself.

To my father, my hero and strong guiding light, Dooj and to Mum, departed but not forgotten. You have both given me a love of reading and learning.

To Kris for support in writing this book; to Emy for design.

We all have many people in our lives, be they family, friends, colleagues and teachers, who make an impact on us in various ways: through gestures of kindness, words of encouragement, wisdom, perspective, stories and knowledge. I am grateful to all of you.

To the many authors of the thousands of books I have read over the years; especially Tom Peters, Wayne Dyer, Stephen Covey, Thich Nhat Hanh, Tim Ferris, Michael Sliwinski, Dale Carnegie, Dave Allen, Ray Dalio, Seth Godin, Daniel Priestley, Phil Jones, Perry Marshall, Abraham Twerski, Bernadette Jiwa, Elizabeth Gilbert, Deepak Chopra, Daniel Kahnemann, Steven Pressfield, Eckart Tolle, Paramhansa Yogananda, Robert Jordan Fritz, Alan Weiss, Cal Newport, Michael Hauge, Robert Cialdini, Michael Watkins, Russ Harris, Allan Dib, Josh Kaufman, Charles Duhigg, Mike Dooley, James Clear, Nir Eyal, Tal Ben Shahar and many others.

TABLE OF CONTENTS

FOREWORD

Of all the many hundreds of people I have coached, it's the ones with so much opportunity at the early stages of their careers, for whom I especially wrote this book. But in reality, this book is for anyone starting a new job.

I am in the advanced stages of my career. I am at the time in my life where I want to and can help as many people as possible.

I feel I can do this better from the perspective of age and experience – looking backwards – rather than looking forwards.

Oscar Wilde said: "Experience is merely the name men gave to their mistakes."

My purpose in writing this book is for you to experience working life more fully and without making the same mistakes that I made.

Ideally, when starting a new job, it's about some key things so you can successfully launch, relaunch or accelerate your career.

I recently received a letter from Tori, 27 years of age, who shared her struggles with starting a new job.

"When I first began my career in buying, I had studied a short course, passed and was offered every job I interviewed for. I felt unstoppable and had friends who had degrees in the subject who were envious of my success. I had always been an A-grade student and everything I went for, I got. I was confident in starting my career, but the realities of the working world hit me quickly.

My new line manager expected so many things from me that I didn't understand or know how to do and didn't have the confidence to admit I didn't know.

I thought admitting that I didn't know meant I wasn't supposed to be in the job, that they'd fire me or I wouldn't even pass the probation period. I'd sit in meetings and feel like I was being spoken to in Japanese. I could not understand a thing and I was too embarrassed to ask anyone.

There were options for training to try and help, but I never wanted to be seen actually taking one of these classes because I felt that meant I might be seen as incapable in the first place.

Quickly I began to drown under the stress and instead of just asking for the help I needed, I chose to jump ship and look for work elsewhere.

I talked my way into a new job with one of the biggest companies in fashion at the time, beating out (apparently 4,000) other applicants.

Unfortunately the job description was misleading. I essentially became a glorified PA. It was a very bad fit. This almost broke me. I believed I had failed once again, despite how much I was told that the company was at fault, even by HR. But I didn't believe them - I thought there was something wrong with me. I stuck it out for 6 months and my confidence withered. Eventually I moved on, to a large fashion retailer. Another incredible opportunity I had been given. I finally understood everything in the meetings; I was in a place to start giving suggestions and feeling like a cog within the team.

This is when I was introduced to office politics. I believed we were all a part of the same team; we all had the same goal, but I was wrong.

People would throw me under the bus to get a little praise regardless of how much I'd helped them previously. They'd take recognition for my work which I didn't mind until I saw that it got them promotions and I was seen as lazy.

I hadn't kissed the right arses, I didn't stay for after work drinks enough.

Staying late after work meant you weren't good enough to do your job in the allotted hours. Leaving too early meant you didn't care about the job and heaven forbid you tried to take your lunch away from your desk.

Once you slipped out of this circle it was next to impossible to claw your way back in. I had been very naive when beginning my career.

All this actually sent me into a deep depression. I almost gave up on my dream."

Tori's recount is an honest, raw and telling insight.

When we met for a chat and I explained the concept of employee onboarding to her and what I do, it dawned on her that she had never been given any onboarding support. She was literally thrown in the deep end.

This book gives you the onboarding support you need so you can become a success in your new job and you don't have to experience what Tori shared.

Greg Weiss

Feb 2019

INTRODUCTION

INTRODUCTION

You've got the job! Congratulations. The tedious process of submitting a job application, acing a series of interviews and surviving reference checks has paid off. It's a step up for you, and you're excited about what's in store for your career.

You're probably thinking about making a great first impression on your new team, hitting that first round of KPIs and improving a stale or fragmented system.

But, there's a problem. You see, there's a good chance you're not even going to survive your probation period - that critical first three months.

Your first three months is the time to prove yourself, to show that you're capable of doing everything you said in your interview, and more. Essentially, it's the time to put your money where your mouth is. But, unfortunately, an astonishing 20% of people fail their trial period[1].

Now, that figure accounts for failure in your employer's eyes. But, what about your own?

Would you be surprised to hear that up to 20% of employee turnover happens within the first 45 days. And that rate can be even higher for Millennials[2].

The truth is, no matter the level of expertise we have or the industry we work in, so many of us are bouncing around from job to job, trying to find that elusive 'perfect fit'.

Have you been there before? That means you've moved through the arduous process of finding a new job only to be out of one a mere six to twelve weeks later. And if you're one of the 20%, this jumping between jobs might be at a cost to your career goals, financial stability and even your sense of self-worth.

We've all felt that it shouldn't be this way.

So, what if I told you that *it doesn't have to be this way*? For any person, in any job, at any level, in any industry.

HOW TO BE SET UP FOR SUCCESS

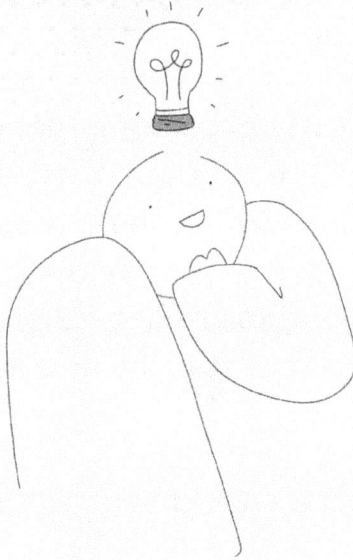

How do I know there's a way to reverse these statistics and find success in your new role?

I've helped thousands of people, just like you, survive the first three months of their job and beyond.

But I've also been where you are. Before I started in the HR business around 30 years ago, I was employed by some large companies in marketing and business development. I never really felt all that connected to my employers, and I rarely felt supported to succeed in my job.

For a long time, I thought the problem must be with me. So I moved from job to job - more often than I would have liked. I often felt unsettled and demoralised. Despite wanting to succeed, I seemed to experience the same problems over and over again at each new job.

It wasn't until years later when I started to look back on my time through an HR lens that I realised some things. You see, in all of these roles, I was either given an extremely short and inadequate orientation or, more commonly, I was simply left to my own devices from day one. Each time I would be left trying to muddle my way through the role.

And my experience certainly isn't an isolated one. I've discovered that most companies do not offer any structured programs to support their employees in their first three months.

Without support in that critical period, employees aren't set up for success. They become disengaged, feeling:

- Overwhelmed and confused about what they are supposed to be doing and who they can talk to for support

- Unsure of any developmental opportunities available to them

- Unable to see where they fit into the big picture of the organisation

- Lacking reward or recognition for their work

Employers often assume disengaged employees are just a 'bad fit' or have poor performance. Sometimes they blame it on generational issues, a lack of loyalty or a flawed recruitment process. They're looking for something to blame because employee turnover comes at a considerable cost - in time, money and effort.

But this causes managers to focus on the immediate, productivity and work-based requirements of employees. That means they're overlooking the other, but equally important side of a disengaged employee - their social, confidence and emotional needs.

So, herein lies the problem. There is a significant disconnect in the *employee-employer experience*. Employers are overlooking the importance of creating a culture that focuses on meeting *all* of the needs of their employees, and, as a result, employee engagement and retention is suffering.

I realised that if employers were to implement a structured three-month onboarding program, they could drastically reduce these issues and employees would have a much higher chance of succeeding in their new role in those first three months and beyond. In fact, research supports this too. Employees whose companies have longer onboarding programs gain full proficiency in their positions 34% faster than those in the shortest programs[3]. And an impressive 69% of employees are more likely to stay with a company for three years thanks to an excellent onboarding experience[4].

Now, I'd like you to take a moment to imagine how it would feel if you could start a new job on the right foot and be set up for success, surviving not just your first three months, but three years or more?

THIS BOOK IS FOR YOU

I've written this book so that you too can benefit from a painless start with a new employer, or in a new position with your current employer. You deserve to have the tools to succeed in your job.

In this book, you'll get to benefit from the insight of the CareerSupport365 three-month onboarding program, based around the acclaimed McKinsey 7-S alignment framework.

This framework proposes seven internal aspects of an organisation that need to be aligned for that business to succeed. However, we believe these same aspects can be applied to employees for their own alignment *within* an organisation. They are summarised as follows:

THE SEVEN STEPS OF SUCCESSFUL ONBOARDING

(1) **Shared values:** Ensure you and your employer's values overlap and identify the behaviours that underpin these values. This is foundational to the success of the onboarding program, the organisation and your own role.

(2) **Structure:** Master the formal and informal structures to ensure you understand the formal reporting lines, as well as the hidden networks for tapping into information and influence.

(3) **Style:** Manage your personal brand to ensure others gain an overwhelmingly positive impression of you.

(4) **Skills:** Apply your unique strengths to your role and minimise your weaknesses for career success.

(5) **Strategy:** Set up 1 or 2 winning projects to energise those around you and build trust, credibility and value.

(6) **Staff:** Learn how to fit and where to contribute by agreeing with your manager on the context of your role.

(7) **Systems:** Get to know the way things work by establishing an accelerated learning agenda so you can contribute effectively.

It's these seven steps of the program that I'm sharing with you in this book.

But, unlike other onboarding practices, this program is designed to eliminate three considerable barriers to success. They are:

- Giving too much information in one go. Instead, you'll receive information that's drip-fed and much easier to digest.

- Forgetting to focus on the human element. I believe productivity is important, but it's not what comes first. Ultimately, you need to feel safe and comfortable in your surroundings.

- Thinking that training constitutes adequate onboarding. Onboarding considers the wider picture of your employment. The little things such as where to find the coffee machine, and understanding the organisational structure are critical to you doing your best work.

What would successful, ongoing employment mean for you? Would it feel as though:

- "I finally 'fit in' at a company."

- "I'm secure in my position, and I don't go to work worrying that I'm going to be fired."

- "I have clarity around my role and KPIs."

- "I'll be able to make quick wins from the outset to impress others and gain confidence."

- "I not only understand my role but the wider business culture."

- "I can enjoy regular, planned holidays, not just the time-off I always seem to have between jobs."

WHO AM I TO HELP YOU?

For most of my working career, I have helped managers and executives accelerate and relaunch their careers.

I am known for being an entrepreneur, especially within the HR profession. I have started (and sold) several HR-related businesses from executive search and recruitment; to employee engagement and retention; to HR Director level development and networking.

Most recently, I founded CareerSupport365 which provides services for employers to successfully onboard their newly appointed employees; and offboarding – also known as outplacement services - that allows departing employees to be equipped with the knowledge, skills and attitudes to work out where they will be happy in their next career move.

I'm proud that 83 percent of participants in our unique offboarding service have successfully re-launched their careers within six weeks of completing their coursework and heeding my advice.

WHY THIS BOOK, WHY NOW?

You might be wondering, why now is the best time to be learning how to make the best of a new role?

Firstly, there's the Millennial mindset. There are currently vast numbers of millennials entering the workforce. And as we've seen, they are more at risk than other generations of leaving a new position in those first 45 days.

Then, there's the myth that the grass is always greener on the other side of the fence. This myth, when compounded with what we see every day on social media plays a significant role in people deciding they should move on to something that's a 'better fit'. Social media presents a glamorised view of some careers, causing us to desire what others have. But, it's always important to remember that what we see isn't necessarily an accurate representation of their 'daily grind'.

And finally, there's the increasing awareness of the role mental health plays in the workplace. As more people every day feel as though they don't fit in, it's essential to show them that the problem isn't with them. We all need to acknowledge that it's worth trying to make a success of each job, we just need a new, more structured and supportive approach.

HOW TO USE THIS BOOK

This book will guide you step by step through the onboarding process you can use to ensure your new role is exactly what you want it to be - a success.

What it isn't, is a book you devour once, put down and expect results. What it is, is a specially-designed process to work through. As you read each chapter, you will find activities to help you implement what you have just read. These are supported by examples and case studies all designed to help you make the most of each new module.

It's essential to complete each one before moving to the next if you are to survive your first three months in a new job.

I wish you well as you read this book and enjoy a higher chance of fitting in and performing in those first three months.

Please let me know how *your* first three months go. Email me at: **gregw@wtfisnext.wtf**

CHAPTER 1

PREPARE FOR BOARDING

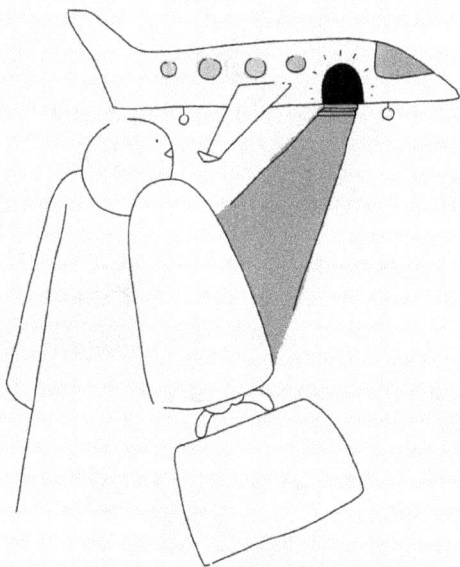

Think back to the last time you were a passenger on a plane. You would have received a ticket, taken directions from the airline crew and followed signage. No matter your destination, there was a defined process to follow to board the plane and find your seat. Then, you were given safety instructions alongside a demonstration "in case of emergency". This set the tone for a safe, successful take off and journey.

This same idea applies to onboarding. It is a structured process for being brought into a new company, department or role, with the aim of giving you the skills, knowledge and context for you to excel.

If you onboard properly, then the experience gives you a good impression of your new employer. And it creates the conditions that are key to increasing the chances of making your career move a real success.

You want that, and your employer wants that too.

That's why this book sets out an onboarding program aiming to:

1. Provide a context of onboarding beyond your own job description, and for the wider business.

2. Manage those first and critical three months.

3. Help you understand the nuances of the business culture.

4. Enable you to network with internal and external stakeholders.

5. Guide you towards making quick wins to impress others and gain confidence.

> "It's about ensuring that employees are able to come to work in the knowledge that there's a safe and supportive work environment. And it's important for employees to have that knowledge, to have that comfort."
>
> **John Studdert**
> *Angel Investor and Business Advisor*

WHAT ONBOARDING IS NOT

It's a common mistake to associate onboarding with orientation or induction. In fact, it is neither of these.

Orientation provides a basic awareness of your employer, while induction tends to focus on workplace health and safety requirements. These practices are usually conducted in a single session or across a relatively short time. Because of their short duration and the tendency to "information dump" on the new employee, the nature of orientation and induction do not encourage employee longevity.

You can see both of these primarily meet the needs of the employer. On the other hand, onboarding provides empowerment *for the employee*. Onboarding isn't about only fulfilling the needs or prerequisites of your employer; it is about achieving success in this new role, for your own benefit as much as theirs. In other words, onboarding is a process that takes time and provides the tools needed for employees to fulfil organisational objectives, in the way of personal, professional and emotional support. Unlike orientation, the onboarding process is typically laid out across a 3-month period. It is a significant time and energy investment. However, it serves a long-term goal: encouraging an employee

to thrive for their job satisfaction, as well as a higher chance of retention.

Now that you're clear on what onboarding is and isn't, let's take a closer look at the breadth of the benefits you can expect to see if you put this book's strategies into play.

ONBOARDING TO MITIGATE PROBATION FAILURE

As a foundation, you can expect to perform your job well if you possess the necessary skills and onboard adequately. But branching out from this, are a wealth of other benefits. So, it isn't only a case of being able to go to work and do your job, but rather, to thrive emotionally and socially while you are doing so.

It's a big mistake to think that productivity is the sole focus of onboarding, at the exclusion of the human side of the equation. And instead, it's worth thinking about it as a cycle from having your social and emotional needs met to experiencing improved engagement and ultimately, better productivity.

You see, it's been found that new employees are often primarily concerned as to who they'll be

33

working with, who they can ask for help and whether they fit in. When these things are taken care of, employees are 54% more engaged[1] (see figure 1-1). And when they are engaged, employees are 15% more productive[2].

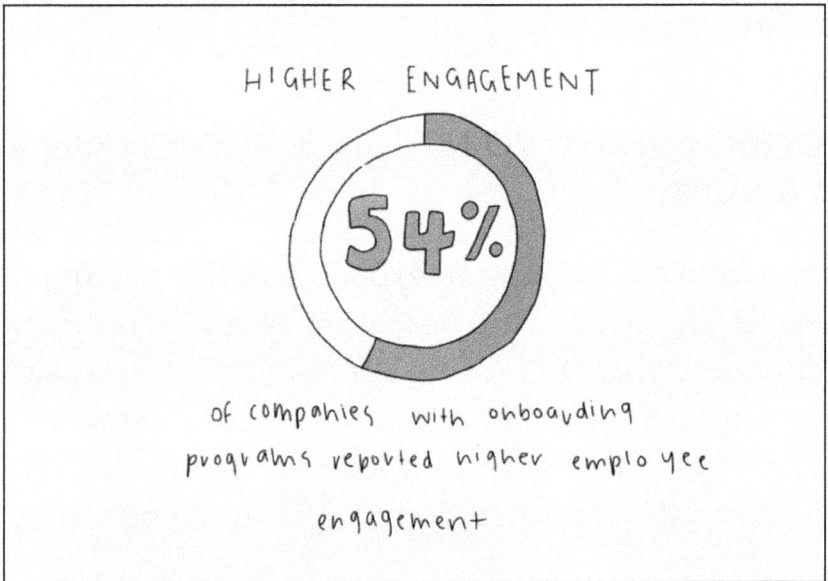

HIGHER ENGAGEMENT

54%

of companies with onboarding programs reported higher employee engagement

Figure 1-1: *Employee engagement for companies with onboarding programs*

It's clear that every new professional role we encounter comes with on-the-job learning curves and of course, we need to master these. But, it's also essential to do so by avoiding debilitating fear and overwhelm. When your needs are addressed on every level, you're assimilated into the organisation

at an accelerated rate, will find yourself able to contribute and become optimally productive much sooner. You'll have clarity around your key competencies, as well as your role, helping with job satisfaction and an increased level of dedication.

By and large, the most significant benefit of successful onboarding is to mitigate the risk of you being one in five people who fail their probation period. Even if you've never fallen to the bottom rung of the ladder before, onboarding poorly puts you at considerable risk.

In fact, often the very nature of the probation period can act against you. You know probation is the time to prove yourself and start showing results so that your employer is compelled to keep you on. So you'll probably feel the pressure because probation seems like a safeguard for employers to easily correct any hiring mistakes they've made (thanks to exclusion from unfair dismissal claims).

Dismissals do still need to comply with local laws, but the probation period is a time of intense uncertainty, often viewed, in effect, as an "employment cooling off period". But, what if you turned it around and started looking at those first three months as a time to grow, to immerse yourself in a new business culture and boost your professional confidence?

That's where some astute planning and self-reflection before you commence onboarding comes into play.

HOW TO PREPARE YOURSELF FOR ONBOARDING

One of the most important things you can do to ensure your onboarding program is a success is to prepare yourself well. Much of this involves looking *within* for a clear understanding of yourself, to guide your approach to your new role.

Mark the transition

Moving out of a role is often stressful as you try to wrap up everything within your power and hand over the reins to those around you. So, it's important to take a breather to prepare yourself mentally for the transition from your previous role to your new one.

It's time to let go of the stresses of the past and start focusing on your future. It's what your new employer will expect, and it's what you owe to yourself too.

You'll ideally have at least a weekend between your roles, so make the most of this time. One thing that can help you make the transition in your mind is to celebrate your new role. Invite family or friends to share in your celebration - particularly those you feel comfortable with, talking about what excites you most about the new position.

Realise your preferences

We'll talk further about applying your unique strengths and minimising your weaknesses. But, it's also prudent to start a new role by being aware of your preferences. Consider the tasks you really enjoy and gravitate towards, as well as those you'd prefer

to avoid. It's important not to neglect those less desirable aspects of a role from the outset.

Remember, if you perform at 100% in two areas and 20% in another two areas, that's only an average of 60%. You need to figure out how you will compensate for those less desirable responsibilities. That could be by planning to carve out a particular amount of time each week to ensure they are completed or finding someone with razor-sharp skills in this area to guide you forward.

Whichever way best suits you to compensate, make sure you have a plan.

Reset bad habits

When you're commencing a new role, it's the ideal time for a fresh start not just in the work you do, or who you're employed by, but for your habits too. After all, it's easy to get into bad habits - especially when the office space easily facilitates those bad habits, like compulsive social media checking.

But, bad habits are not just around your use of social media. It's also about a range of things from how often you engage in friendly chit-chat to your inclination to multi-task. When it's happening too often, it can mean that our attention is split between too many tasks, rather than focusing on just the one. It can also lead to feeling overwhelmed, overworked and less inclined to engage in productive work.

Move past reactivity

Like multitasking, reactivity is a significant killer of productivity. The demand we feel always to be responding to others and putting out fires cuts into our productivity in a big way. Of course, these things can't be ignored continually, but it's worth assessing your current levels of reactivity.

Try finding ways to limit those behaviours. For example, having set times to answer emails means that you can have large chunks of time to be proactive and reach peak productivity.

Embrace a learning mindset

No matter how experienced you are, there is always some learning associated with a new role. When you're used to being at the top of your game, the need to suddenly be open to learning can leave you feeling vulnerable.

Early missteps or setbacks can shake your confidence and find you questioning whether this was a good career change after all. Conversely, you may wall up, become defensive and refuse to acknowledge your failures. These behaviours only serve to create tension with your colleagues and superiors.

These outcomes sit at opposite ends of the spectrum, with neither of them ideal. But, if you prepare yourself for learning, you'll take on a more balanced approach that will benefit you in terms of productivity, but also to fit into the social structure of your work environment.

Establish your network

Once you've prepared yourself mentally, it's essential to have a trusted network to rely on for help. When you commence work, it's a given that you will be surrounded by new colleagues and superiors who will be equipped to answer many of your questions. But, it can also be an incredible confidence boost to know you have an external network you can turn to should the need arise.

This is very important when it comes to traversing organisational politics, but also in keeping your own equilibrium. Before you even start your new role, think about who you already know that will be able to assist you in different areas of your professional life.

Each of these areas of preparation will equip you with a strong foundation for starting your new position *and* your onboarding program. This is crucial because the most often cited reasons for failing probation are poor fit, performance, absence, work behaviours and personality clashes (see figure

1-2) [4]. As you can see, many of these are within your control.

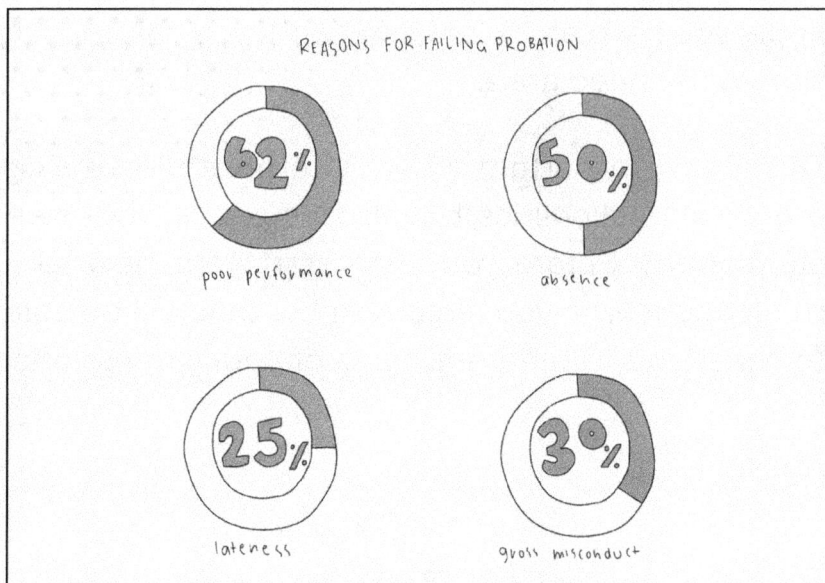

REASONS FOR FAILING PROBATION

62%
poor performance

50%
absence

25%
lateness

3%
gross misconduct

Figure 1-2: *Reasons for failing probation*

So the question is how can you avoid failing your probation period because of these factors?

The good news is, it's largely in your hands. If you take control of your own onboarding, you can mitigate the risks and surge ahead for a successful transition.

ACTION STEPS

Note that most of the reasons for termination are like unforced errors in sport - they are avoidable own goals or nets.

So, how do you think *you* can avoid failing your first three months in each of these areas:

1. Performance

_____
_____
_____
_____
_____
_____

2. Fit

_____
_____
_____
_____
_____
_____

3. Absence

_____
_____
_____
_____
_____
_____

4. Poor work behaviours

_____
_____
_____
_____
_____
_____

5. Personality clashes?

_____
_____
_____
_____
_____
_____

KEY LESSONS

Before you proceed to your roadmap for onboarding, I encourage you to revisit some key points from the chapter you just read:

The onboarding process is not an orientation or induction as often thought. Instead, it is typically a 3-month process that brings you into a new company, department or role. Onboarding aims to equip you with the skills, knowledge and context for you to excel in your new position. When you onboard well, it gives you a good impression of your employer, and likewise, for them a good impression of you.

The onboarding process can help your employer meet your social and emotional needs so that you become an engaged employee, and ultimately, a productive and contributing member of the team. But, first and foremost, a structured onboarding process will help to mitigate your 1-in-5 risk of failing probation.

To prepare yourself for onboarding successfully, I suggest you:

1. Mark the transition by letting go of your past role and celebrating the new.

2. Realise your preferences, so you can compensate for areas you're likely to neglect.

3. Reset bad habits to reduce the chances of overwhelm and doing unproductive work.

4. Move past reactivity by limiting 'busy work' behaviours to reach peak productivity.

5. Embrace a learning mindset to help you fit into your new environment.

6. Establish your network externally, so that you feel supported and confident in your new role.

32% of global executives in a Korn/Ferry survey rate the onboarding they experienced as below average or poor [5]. With this book, you don't need to rely on your employer implementing an outstanding structured onboarding program. So, prepare yourself well, approach it in the right manner and you *won't* be one of the 32%.

Good luck - it's in your hands.

CHAPTER 2

A ROADMAP TO ONBOARDING WITHIN THE MCKINSEY 7-S FRAMEWORK

According to Andrew O'Keeffe, author of Hardwired Humans [1], we can learn much about maintaining organizational harmony by observing chimp communities.

For example, when a newly introduced chimp lacks the necessary social skills to be mindful of group dynamics, it is at risk of being attacked or even killed. Strangers are not easily welcomed into chimp communities, lest they upset the social hierarchy.

Is this starting to sound familiar?

It's been said that joining a new company is akin to a chimp being introduced into a new community. And much like an introduced chimp, if you are not thoughtful in adapting to your new situation, you could end up being the subject of hostility and rejected.

With that picture in mind, consider what HR practitioners believe: if you are a new employee recruited from outside the organisation you will face more challenges than someone who received a promotion from within.

As an outside hire, you are more at risk of failure because:

- Clarity around your role is likely to become murkier before it becomes clearer

- You are facing a corporate culture different from the one you experienced previously

- You are unknown, so face developing entirely new relationships and overcoming a perceived lack of credibility

- You do not understand the organisation's flow of communication, money or information, both internally and externally

But, you can take action on all of these fronts to minimise risk and give yourself the best chance of thriving in your new role.

> "Workplaces are not our natural habitat. This gives a lot of insights into why people think and act the way they do."
>
> **Andrew O'Keefe**
> *Author & Director*

THE 4 FOUNDATIONAL ELEMENTS OF ONBOARDING SUCCESSFULLY

The McKinsey 7-S model provides your roadmap to overcoming each of the barriers by mastering the four foundational elements of onboarding (see figure 2-1).

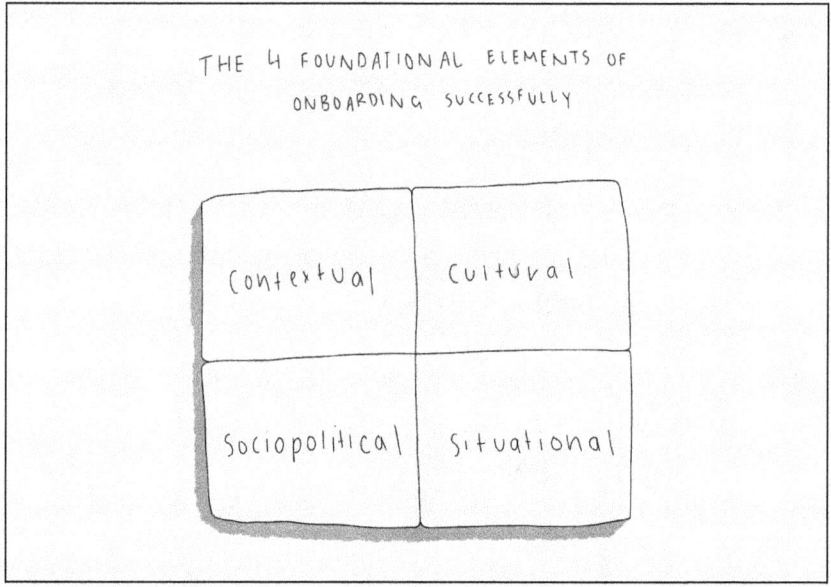

THE 4 FOUNDATIONAL ELEMENTS OF ONBOARDING SUCCESSFULLY

Contextual	Cultural
Sociopolitical	Situational

Figure 2-1: Four foundational elements of successful onboarding.

1. Contextual

When you start a new job, understandings you formed in those early, heady days of being recruited are often discovered to be less accurate.

You see, the context of your employment often moulds your employer's expectations of your performance in your new role. But, when you are initially employed, you are often unaware of exactly what this context is and how it translates into the reality of working in your new role. This means that once you start employment and the context becomes more evident, you must take into account what or who has come before you.

According to CEB's study of High-Impact Leadership Transitions[2], you may be employed under one of five contexts:

Smooth Sailing—*The leader moves into a position according to a previously arranged transition plan under normal business conditions (3% of leadership transitions).*

Replacing an Icon—*The leader's predecessor was very successful in the job (18%).*

Following a Train Wreck—*The leader's predecessor was not successful in the job (27%).*

Jump Start—*A static environment where the performance of the leader's predecessor wasn't particularly strong or weak, but the organization needs to quickly move in a different direction (19%).*

Breaking Ground—The leader assumes a newly created position (31%).

Using this lens, it's clear that there are few easy transitions: less than 3% of transitioning leaders can look forward to a high degree of role clarity and modest pressure for results in their new roles.

It's critical you face up to the reality of the situation that greets you as you begin your new role. Adjust your expectations to meet those of the position and your employer accordingly.

2. Cultural

You can think about the business culture as its "personality". This makes it harder to grasp when you enter a new workplace as it is less tangible than formal business structures.

Workplace culture is sometimes allowed to develop naturally. However, research by Deloitte[3] shows that companies with strong, defined workplace cultures are believed to be more successful, and have happier and more satisfied employees. With this in mind, you can see how vital a strong workplace culture can be to an organisation overall, but also to you, as you progress through your career with this new employer.

Much like your own professional development, you should expect the organisation's culture to be a work-in-progress. And remember that it may differ between departments and divisions.

To adapt successfully, there are a few best practices to follow:

- Follow the lead of your colleagues in the early days

- Be open-minded to suggestions and approaches made by your colleagues and managers

- Share your knowledge, while being mindful not to force it on others

- Take note of things that are challenging for the team, and then take time to understand why they are that way before you suggest changes to the relevant processes

When you are secure in your position, with a good understanding of the business culture, you will be able to create more flexibility around making changes to the way things are done. You'll learn further about this in Chapter 4 (Structure).

3. Socio-political

You must develop the right relationships as soon as possible to position you for success not only during the critical onboarding period but throughout your tenure with the organisation and beyond. It might not be the people most obvious to you who you need to build working relationships with.

Indeed, you can never predict who will be instrumental to your success now, or further into your career. In five or even ten years, someone you work with now could be the person who hires you, recommends you, or builds an entirely new business with you. Peers and those in supporting roles can be just as influential when it comes to your day-to-day life at work, as your superiors.

Relationship-building requires a significant time investment on your part, but an organisation is a team environment, so it's essential you do so. After all, it's impossible to "go it alone."

You should connect with co-workers in both formal and informal settings. If you're looking for ways to make introductions, mention this to your colleagues so they can help to facilitate those new connections. You can also offer to sit in on some additional meetings. You might not be in a position to contribute directly, but it's an ideal way to both show your interest in other aspects of the business while getting exposure to those outside your routine interactions.

You'll dive deeper into relationship-building and navigating the political environment in Chapter 7 (Strategy) and Chapter 8 (Staff).

4. Situational

This element of onboarding should be the easiest to master in your first three months. The situational aspects of your new employer relate to their offerings, how they communicate internally and externally, their position in the industry and their operational structure. You must understand not only where you fit as a single employee, but where your department fits and where the company sits in the market, locally and globally.

To demonstrate this further, let's look at a specific example. Imagine you are a newly-hired marketing department manager. You focus solely on running your department well but fail to consider the context of where your department sits within the business. You start pursuing a new marketing strategy

without informing the sales team. Communication channels between departments break down and a rift forms. The sales and marketing strategies are now misaligned. As a result, the performance of both departments suffer, and sales projections begin to plummet.

This rift has arisen purely from a lack of context of where your department is situated in the business and how it is meant to communicate with other departments. You'll have the chance to address this further in subsequent chapters, but for now, I'd like you to consider whether you have the following understanding of your employer's organisation. Remember to think across all levels, from customers to teams, departments to the entire company and at an industry level. For instance:

- Where does your employer sit in the market?

- Who are their competitors?

- What is their USP and in what way does this differentiate them?

- How do they communicate internally with each other, and externally with customers?

ACTION STEPS

1. Contextual

Identify the context of your transition. Recheck your job description and make peace with any difference between the expectations you are now aware of, compared to those you held initially.

_____

_____

_____

_____

_____

_____

2. Cultural

In what area do you think you might need to exercise the most restraint, in terms of being open-minded and taking the lead of your colleagues? Hint: think about your bugbears in your previous position.

_____

_____

_____

_____

_____

_____

3. Socio-political

In the past, have you focused on developing relationships primarily with your superiors? How might you approach relationship-building more broadly in future?

_____

_____

_____

_____

_____

_____

4. Situational

What questions can you ask your manager and colleagues about your employer's purpose and their business model – namely how the pieces fit together regarding workflow, and how communication and even money flows in and out.

_____

_____

_____

_____

_____

_____

Now that you have an understanding of the four foundational elements of onboarding successfully let's look at how the McKinsey 7-S alignment framework will be applied to help you master them.

FOUNDATIONS OF THE MCKINSEY 7-S FRAMEWORK

The conception of this acclaimed framework dates back to the late 1970's, but it has never lost relevance. In fact, it is an organisational framework that has not only endured over time but continues to inform management thinking.

The basic premise of the McKinsey & Co 7-S framework is that there are seven internal aspects of an organisation that need to be aligned, for it to be successful (see figure 2-2). It's crucial to realise that the model does not address organisational structure, but the role of *coordination* in organisational effectiveness.

In fact, Lowell Bryan, a director in McKinsey's New York office, likens the framework to the Knights of the Round Table [4]. For there is no hierarchy, or pyramid of power, no head nor foot, only *collaboration*. This makes it possible to uncover blind spots within an organisation. It also means that an organisation can't make significant progress without some progress in all of the seven areas. Each of the seven internal aspects of effectiveness *reinforces* the other.

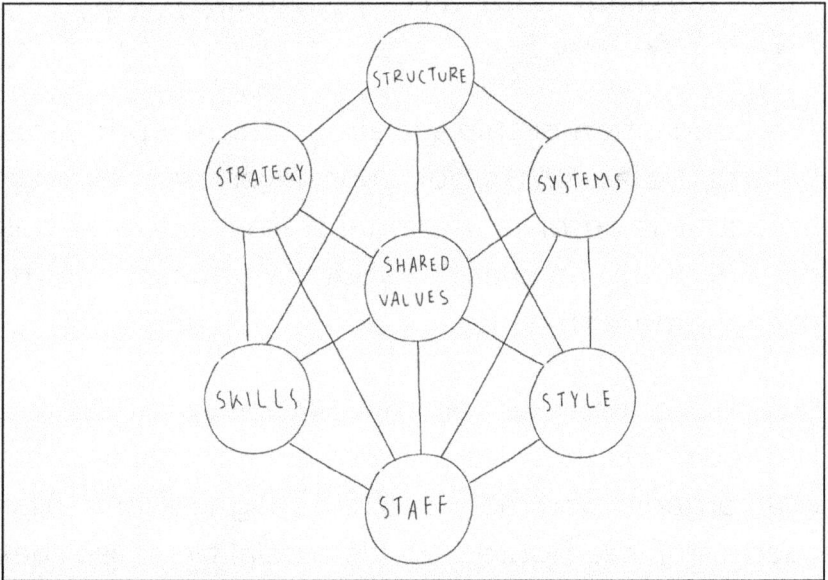

Figure 2-2: *The McKinsey & Co 7-S framework*

The McKinsey 7-S framework can be applied to any aspect of organisational and team effectiveness - it is particularly useful during times of change. And it has been proven to perform well in identifying what needs to be realigned or to maintain alignment.

Therefore, it stands to reason that the framework

can be applied by you, an employee transitioning into a new role, for your own alignment to the organisation during this time of change.

You will learn to apply the framework by following three foundational steps:

1. You analyse the current situation and ask the right questions throughout the onboarding process. You will direct questions inward, but also externally to the organisation.

2. You identify the ideal future situation and any inconsistencies between the two positions.

3. You make alignment choices to negate these inconsistencies and move towards your goal of achieving a successful career transition.

So, let me introduce you to the 7-S's, the aspects of this framework that will guide you through the onboarding process.

UNDERSTANDING THE 7-S'S FOR ALIGNMENT

Although equally weighted, the seven aspects of this model fall into two categories: objective and subjective, as illustrated in figure 2-3.

The objective category includes Systems, Strategy and Structure. These are the easier ones to identify and define, encompassing formal processes and reporting lines.

The subjective aspects are Shared Values, Style, Skills and Staff. They are less tangible and more influenced by culture.

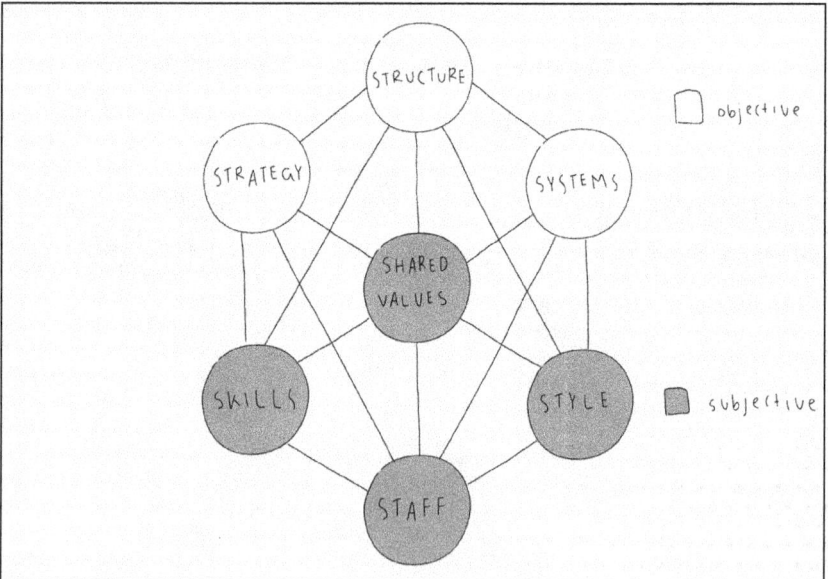

Figure 2-3: *The McKinsey 7-S framework: objective and subjective aspects*

It's worth noting that the original version of the framework considered systems to be a subjective aspect of an organisation. However, over time, organisational processes have been documented and automated to the point where they are easy to analyse and thus have been reclassified as objective.

As you move through the following chapters, each of the 7-S aspects will be defined and explained before you are prompted to make your own alignment choice relevant to each one.

THE SEVEN STEPS OF SUCCESSFUL ONBOARDING

(1) **Shared values:** Ensure you and your employer's values overlap and identify the behaviours that underpin these values. This is foundational to the success of the onboarding program, the organisation and your own role.

(2) **Structure:** Master the formal and informal structures to ensure you understand the formal reporting lines, as well as the hidden networks for tapping into information and influence.

(3) **Style:** Manage your personal brand to ensure others gain an overwhelmingly positive impression of you.

(4) **Skills:** Apply your unique strengths to your role and minimise your weaknesses for career success.

(5) **Strategy:** Set up 1 or 2 winning projects to energise those around you and build trust, credibility and value.

(6) **Staff:** Learn how to fit and where to contribute by agreeing with your manager on the context of your role.

(7) **Systems:** Get to know the way things work by establishing an accelerated learning agenda so you can contribute effectively.

KEY LESSONS

As you use this framework to try to adapt to your new workplace and position, I encourage you to take the time to reflect at the end of each chapter.

Keep in mind these lessons from the chapter you've just read:

By mastering the four foundational elements of successful onboarding, you'll gain a clear understanding of the wider business, and form connections that will help to support you during your time in this position and beyond. Remember to seek relationships at all levels.

Not every job or employer are as they seem during the recruitment stage. You'll need to adjust your expectations to align with the reality of your early employment and, most importantly, the context of your transition.

Finding an in-road to the workplace culture may be the biggest challenge you face, but it is by no means insurmountable. Take your cue from the behaviours and communications occurring around you as you settle in.

A ROADMAP TO ONBOARDING WITHIN THE MCKINSEY 7-S FRAMEWORK

To achieve these results, you'll be making seven alignment choices to represent the objective and subjective aspects of the McKinsey 7-S framework:

- Shared values
- Structure
- Style
- Skills
- Strategy
- Staff
- Systems

You'll be guided to make each alignment choice by following three foundational steps:

1. You analyse the current situation and ask the right questions throughout the onboarding process.

2. You identify the ideal future situation and any inconsistencies between the two positions.

3. You make alignment choices to negate these inconsistencies.

Chapter 3 brings your first alignment choice from the central aspect of the model: Shared values.

CHAPTER 3

SHARED VALUES

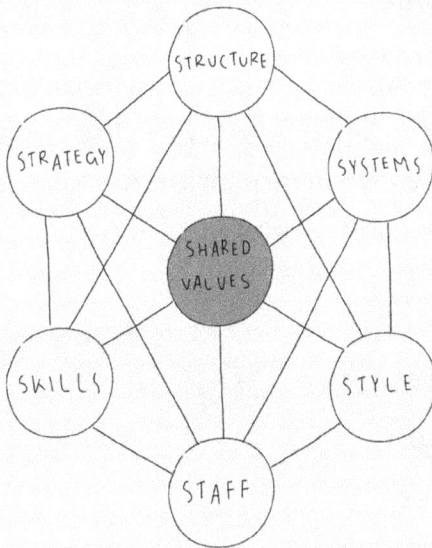

You can see that Shared Values take pride of place in the centre of the McKinsey 7-S framework and therefore our onboarding framework. That's because values are critical to the successful alignment of all other aspects. Each of the six remaining aspects stem from what the organisation you are employed by stands for. They are so interwoven with the organisational values, that, should those core values change, then Style, Skills, Staff, Systems, Strategy and Structure would all need to transform to reflect the altered values.

But, in general, organisational core values do not change. They are timeless, holding steadfast for the long-term. Every organisation's core values tend to relate to four main areas of business:

- People
- Customers
- Products
- Processes

Typically, they focus on how people are expected to connect to each other, as well as the way they should be treated so they can do their best work. Values go one powerful step further than morals. While morals will relate to how people *intend* to behave, values

influence how people *actually do* behave.

It's a common misconception that skills outweigh values when it comes to the workplace. But, while you can acquire skills and knowledge in a relatively short amount of time, values are more ingrained, forming the foundation of everyday behaviours.

This is why your recommended first alignment choice is:

- **To ensure your values and your employer's values overlap**

"We're more encouraged when we're recruiting to the values and the culture of the organisation than recruiting to the skills. We can teach skills. If you can get the culture and value part, it doesn't matter how clever you are with the skills part."

Peter Lancken
Chairman & Director

BENEFITS OF VALUES ALIGNMENT IN THE WORKPLACE

All relationships that stand the test of time are founded in shared values - marriages, friendships, partnerships, rock bands and of course, the employee/employer relationship.

According to Ian Boreham[1], three key areas of values alignment can impact in the long-term (see figure 3-1):

- Work attitudes
- Turnover
- Prosocial behavior

Figure 3-1: *Three key areas impacted by values alignment according to Ian Boreham.*

As you explore them below, try to think back to a previous position you held, where your connection to the organisation's values benefited you in each of these areas.

Work attitudes

When you have strong values alignment with your employer, it fosters the more intangible aspects of employee engagement. For instance, your level of motivation, commitment and job satisfaction tend to increase. You also enjoy greater feelings of personal success.

Turnover

The natural progression from having positive work attitudes is that you are more likely to enjoy your job, feeling an affinity with your employer and a sense of cohesion with your team. When this happens, you are more likely to remain with the company, reducing the risk of turnover.

Prosocial behaviours

Strong values alignment positively influences your organisational citizenship behaviours. You'll take part in teamwork and behave in a cooperative, rather than competitive manner. You'll be more inclined to share resources for the better functioning of your team and the wider organisation.

The key to all these benefits arising from shared values is employee engagement. You've already read about the intangible side of this, but the tangible effects of engagement are visible in your direct work output and activities. In short, your productivity and success in the role are greater.

During the time you remain in one role, you are bound to come up against new challenges and be required to learn new skills. The interesting thing is that your job satisfaction and engagement has less to do with the actual work and more to do with how you feel about the work you're doing.

When employees can identify what an organisation, as a whole, cares about, and can align their own values to this, it helps the organisation achieve its core mission. It means you hold each other accountable to these shared values, strengthening the fabric of the organisation. Everyone works toward common goals, understanding each other and building excellent working relationships.

Conversely, when your values are out of alignment, you risk working toward the wrong goals, putting morale and job satisfaction in jeopardy. With misaligned intentions, all decisions you make in the workplace will also be out of alignment. These kinds of reactive choices only serve to compromise company values, adversely affecting the company, and your career too. A small consequence of values misalignment could see you fail your probation period. The largest consequence - a department ends up off-track, or it corrupts an entire brand.

When you align your value system with the company's, it allows for proactive decision-making from a place of understanding.

IDENTIFYING PERSONAL VALUES

Now that you are clear on the *why* of values alignment, it's time to drill down and pinpoint what your values are.

Rather than trying to come up with values from thin air, you'll find a comprehensive list of 418 values following. I have reproduced it here for your ease of use. This list has been compiled by Steve Pavlina[2], which you can also access here if you prefer: *https://www.stevepavlina.com/blog/2004/11/list-of-values/*

Abundance	Affection	Articulacy
Acceptance	Affluence	Artistry
Accessibility	Aggressiveness	Assertiveness
Accomplishment	Agility	Assurance
Accountability	Alertness	Attentiveness
Accuracy	Altruism	Attractiveness
Achievement	Amazement	Audacity
Acknowledgement	Ambition	Availability
Activeness	Amusement	Awareness
Adaptability	Anticipation	Awe
Adoration	Appreciation	Balance
Adroitness	Approachability	Beauty
Advancement	Approval	Being the best
Adventure	Art	Belonging

Benevolence
Bliss
Boldness
Bravery
Brilliance
Buoyancy
Calmness
Camaraderie
Candor
Capability
Care
Carefulness
Celebrity
Certainty
Challenge
Change
Charity
Charm
Chastity
Cheerfulness
Clarity
Cleanliness
Clear-mindedness
Cleverness
Closeness
Comfort
Commitment
Community
Compassion
Competence
Competition
Completion
Composure
Concentration
Confidence
Conformity
Congruency
Connection
Consciousness
Conservation
Consistency
Contentment

Continuity
Contribution
Control
Conviction
Conviviality
Coolness
Cooperation
Cordiality
Correctness
Country
Courage
Courtesy
Craftiness
Creativity
Credibility
Cunning
Curiosity
Daring
Decisiveness
Decorum
Deference
Delight
Dependability
Depth
Desire
Determination
Devotion
Devoutness
Dexterity
Dignity
Diligence
Direction
Directness
Discipline
Discovery
Discretion
Diversity
Dominance
Dreaming
Drive
Duty
Dynamism

Eagerness
Ease
Economy
Ecstasy
Education
Effectiveness
Efficiency
Elation
Elegance
Empathy
Encouragement
Endurance
Energy
Enjoyment
Entertainment
Enthusiasm
Environmentalism
Ethics
Euphoria
Excellence
Excitement
Exhilaration
Expectancy
Expediency
Experience
Expertise
Exploration
Expressiveness
Extravagance
Extroversion
Exuberance
Fairness
Faith
Fame
Family
Fascination
Fashion
Fearlessness
Ferocity
Fidelity
Fierceness
Financial independence

SHARED VALUES

Firmness
Fitness
Flexibility
Flow
Fluency
Focus
Fortitude
Frankness
Freedom
Friendliness
Friendship
Frugality
Fun
Gallantry
Generosity
Gentility
Giving
Grace
Gratitude
Gregariousness
Growth
Guidance
Happiness
Harmony
Health
Heart
Helpfulness
Heroism
Holiness
Honesty
Honor
Hopefulness
Hospitality
Humility
Humor
Hygiene
Imagination
Impact
Impartiality
Independence
Individuality
Industry

Influence
Ingenuity
Inquisitiveness
Insightfulness
Inspiration
Integrity
Intellect
Intelligence
Intensity
Intimacy
Intrepidness
Introspection
Introversion
Intuition
Intuitiveness
Inventiveness
Investing
Involvement
Joy
Judiciousness
Justice
Keenness
Kindness
Knowledge
Leadership
Learning
Liberation
Liberty
Lightness
Liveliness
Logic
Longevity
Love
Loyalty
Majesty
Making a difference
Marriage
Mastery
Maturity
Meaning
Meekness
Mellowness

Meticulousness
Mindfulness
Modesty
Motivation
Mysteriousness
Nature
Neatness
Nerve
Nonconformity
Obedience
Open-mindedness
Openness
Optimism
Order
Organization
Originality
Outdoors
Outlandishness
Outrageousness
Partnership
Patience
Passion
Peace
Perceptiveness
Perfection
Perkiness
Perseverance
Persistence
Persuasiveness
Philanthropy
Piety
Playfulness
Pleasantness
Pleasure
Poise
Polish
Popularity
Potency
Power
Practicality
Pragmatism
Precision

Preparedness
Presence
Pride
Privacy
Proactivity
Professionalism
Prosperity
Prudence
Punctuality
Purity
Rationality
Realism
Reason
Reasonableness
Recognition
Recreation
Refinement
Reflection
Relaxation
Reliability
Relief
Religiousness
Reputation
Resilience
Resolution
Resolve
Resourcefulness
Respect
Responsibility
Rest
Restraint
Reverence
Richness
Rigor
Sacredness
Sacrifice
Sagacity
Saintliness
Sanguinity
Satisfaction
Science
Security

Self-control
Selflessness
Self-reliance
Self-respect
Sensitivity
Sensuality
Serenity
Service
Sexiness
Sexuality
Sharing
Shrewdness
Significance
Silence
Silliness
Simplicity
Sincerity
Skillfulness
Solidarity
Solitude
Sophistication
Soundness
Speed
Spirit
Spirituality
Spontaneity
Spunk
Stability
Status
Stealth
Stillness
Strength
Structure
Success
Support
Supremacy
Surprise
Sympathy
Synergy
Teaching
Teamwork
Temperance

Thankfulness
Thoroughness
Thoughtfulness
Thrift
Tidiness
Timeliness
Traditionalism
Tranquility
Transcendence
Trust
Trustworthiness
Truth
Understanding
Unflappability
Uniqueness
Unity
Usefulness
Utility
Valor
Variety
Victory
Vigor
Virtue
Vision
Vitality
Vivacity
Volunteering
Warmheartedness
Warmth
Watchfulness
Wealth
Willfulness
Willingness
Winning
Wisdom
Wittiness
Wonder
Worthiness
Youthfulness
Zeal

ACTION STEPS

1. Choose your contenders

Start by reading through the entire list, circling each value that means something to you. Ideally, you should come up with a list of 30-40 values at this point.

2. Narrow it down

Now it's time to finetune it. Narrow your list down to a more manageable 5-7 values that you would prioritise above all others. If you find you have two or three values that are nearly identical, try to just choose one as a representative.

3. Define your values

Once you have your shortlist, it's time to create your own definition for each value. This is an important step because one value can mean different things to different people. For example, the value of 'Giving' means different things to different people.

One person might define Giving as the act of providing charity to worthy causes or those less fortunate; whereas another might think Giving means being supportive, devoted or kind.

4. Come up with at least one behaviour that helps make it clear to you when each value is being expressed

The main point is to define whatever your value means to you. You'll find some examples below to start you off.

Is one of your core values accountability?

A possible definition: that accountability requires you to take ownership of responsibilities and be answerable for their progress.

The related behaviour: that your team members report weekly to you, to share the progress of a particular task or project, so that you may then provide your own progress report to the CEO.

Is one of your core values safety?

A possible definition: to prevent injury or danger

The related behaviour: to report any hazard immediately for correction and also to alert your colleagues appropriately for their safety until it is rectified.

Is one of your core values appreciation?

Your definition might be: to express gratitude in return for assistance.

The related behaviour: to thank those who help you or those who go the extra mile with a given task.

Value _____

Definition of that value _____

Behaviours that underpin this value for you:

_____
_____
_____
_____
_____
_____

Values are the foundation of a successful career move. Once you are clearer on your own values then you are able to make a more informed decision on the likelihood of an overlap or mismatch with an employer – which we will explore next.

IDENTIFYING YOUR EMPLOYER'S VALUES

So now that you have worked out your 5 - 7 values it's time to see whether you share those values with your employer. That's why Shared Values is at the centre of the McKinsey 7-S framework.

As you would expect, the more that they are shared, the greater the fit.

ACTION STEPS

1. List the values you know your employer to have. Values are often clear from their mission statement or employee handbook, but it's also worth asking directly for those values.

2. For each of your employer's values write down the official definition and even your manager's definition of each.

3. Finally, come up with at least one behaviour that helps make it clear to you when each value is being expressed.

Value _____

Definition of that value _____

Behaviours that underpin this value for you:

_____

_____

_____

_____

_____

_____

CREATING VALUES ALIGNMENT

Now that you understand the values you and your employer hold, it's time to see where those values overlap and how you can create further alignment. It's possible that you have at least one or two shared values, whether these are identical or even just related values. However, it's possible that others will differ.

If you want to enjoy an onboarding process that will see you succeed with your new employer, then you need to make the choice to *create* alignment. This doesn't require you to change your entire value set to fit with your employer, by disregarding what is important to you. But you should emphasise the values you share and gain a greater understanding

of those that represent your employer, but weren't on your list. By giving these values your attention, you can start to work out how you can exhibit behaviours in the workplace that underpin these values, and make decisions that reinforce alignment.

> "Why am I doing this work? How does that add value to the organisation? If you keep that at the centre of what you're doing then you're gonna have a better run"
>
> **Kirby Grattan**
> *HR leader*

WHERE VALUES MEET NEEDS

In 1943, Abraham Maslow published his paper *A Theory of Human Motivation* in which he introduced his hierarchy of needs. His hierarchy is divided into five sections: physiological needs, safety needs, love/belonging needs, esteem needs and self-actualisation needs (see figure 3-2). By working up the pyramid and satisfying each of the needs, humans can be satisfied, successful and content.

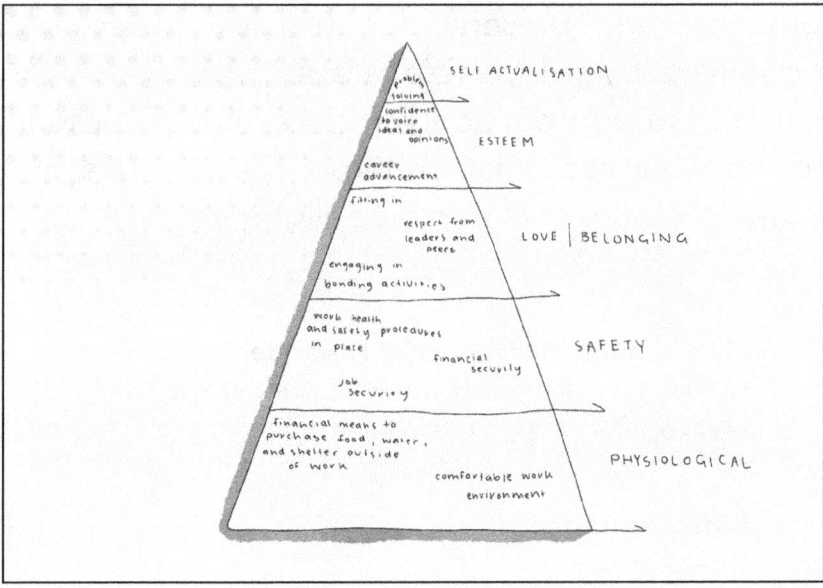

Figure 3-2: *Maslow's hierarchy of needs, adapted for the workplace.*

Interestingly, by aligning your values to that of your employer, you are following a similar upward trend towards greater engagement in the workplace and a level of satisfaction. If you take a look at our representation of Maslow's hierarchy, you can see a strong correlation between the needs described and some of the values mentioned in Steve Pavlina's comprehensive list of values.

Consider this: You have a shared value of community with your employer. This exhibits as a team-oriented and supportive working environment, manifesting in behaviours like offering to help an overloaded

colleague and sharing recognition with your team. Not only does this help the organisation achieve their goals more smoothly, but it also satisfies your mid-level need of love/belonging. Therefore, we can see that values and needs reinforce each other for the ultimate goal of employee engagement.

In fact, the Oxford Handbook of Organisational Psychology [3] cites four essential needs that are crucial for a structured onboarding program.

They are:

1. **The need to belong** which refers to humans' desire to develop robust interpersonal relationships.

2. **Social exchange theory** says our social behaviour and relationships are an exchange process which facilitates a person's perception of who they are within a group.

3. **Uncertainty reduction theory** says we try to reduce uncertainty about others by gaining information about them to help us develop a sense of belonging. Improved interactions can also hasten productivity.

4. **Social identity theory** refers to a person's sense of belonging based on their perception of who they are within a group.

You can see that each of these needs has strong ties to the tiers in Maslow's hierarchy, from Safety, through to Self-actualisation. This tells us that an onboarding program centred around shared values provides you with the best chance of surviving the critical first three months and achieving your subsequent career goals.

KEY LESSONS

As you make the alignment choice for shared values, I encourage you to revisit these lessons from the chapter you just read:

Values form the foundation of everyday behaviours and are more powerful within organisations than morals (which relate more to intentions) and hold more weight than skills (which can be learned more quickly.)

Values provide purpose and motivation. They determine your priorities and are the reasons behind why you think, communicate and act the way you do.

Strong values alignment results in positive work attitudes, increased job satisfaction and improved organisational citizenship behaviours. Alignment helps you to make better, proactive decisions during your workday. Ultimately, it leads to increased fulfilment for you and more impressive results for your employer.

So that you have the best chance of feeling like you are at home while you are at work ensure you have answers to the following:

(1) What your employer's and your own values are

(2) What each of them means to your employer and you

(3) The *behaviours* that underpin these *organisationally* and the *behaviours* that underpin these for you *personally*

(4) How to align your values more closely with those of your employer

Remember that people define values differently, so it's important to speak to your employer directly for clarification on how these values could manifest in your new workplace.

Chapter 4 brings your second alignment choice from one of the objective aspects of the framework: Structure.

CHAPTER 4

STRUCTURE

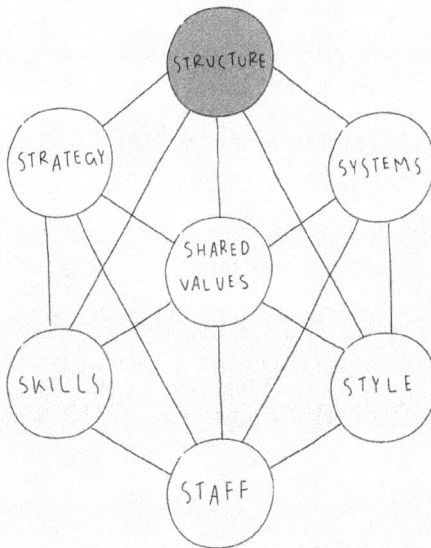

We can learn much about the nature of an organisation by observing an iceberg. For, what is not immediately apparent, is that only 10% of the iceberg is visible above the water, with the rest (90%) hidden below.

It has been said that understanding the depth of an organisation's structure is much like fathoming the deceptive structure of an iceberg (see figure 4-1). Structure demonstrates the placement of individuals, departments and leadership in relation to each other. What you see at a surface level are the objective elements of structure – like the formal reporting lines you see represented in an organisational chart.

But those are just the tip of the iceberg. Under the surface are the informal structures, where you'll discover hidden networks which facilitate the exchange of information and influence.

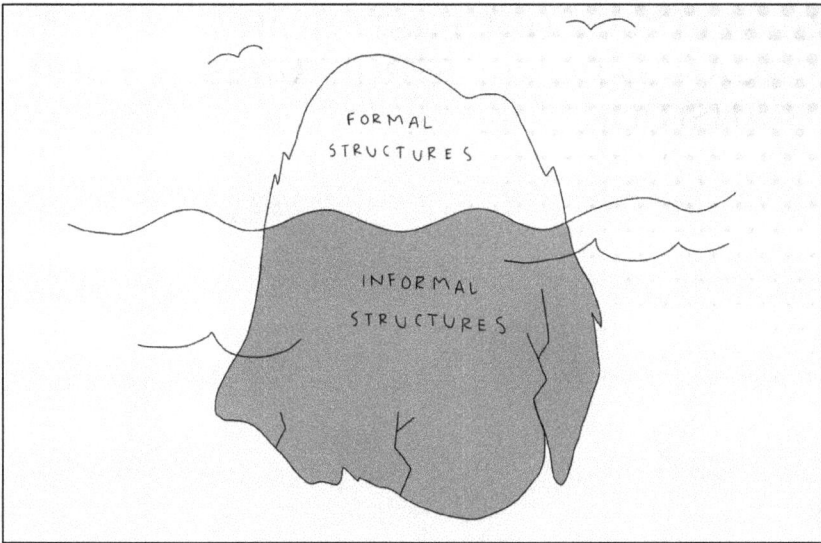

Figure 4-1: *Organisational structure is like that of an iceberg.*

As you can see, although the highly visible core of Structure is objective, it is a unique element within the McKinsey 7-S framework, for it has subjective factors too. Early in your onboarding, it's essential you work out where the pieces fit. This isn't something that necessarily happens overnight, but exploring it now will help your understanding of the organisation's structure, and develop quicker as you proceed through onboarding.

This is why your recommended second alignment choice is:

- **To master the formal and informal structures**

BENEFITS OF UNDERSTANDING ORGANISATIONAL STRUCTURES IN YOUR TRANSITION

Grasping the way formal and informal structures work, acts to break down some of the barriers you may experience as a new hire. In particular, it helps you to:

- Communicate effectively

- Understand who to go to with a specific problem

- Have confidence when approaching new colleagues

- Save time by not seeking help where it won't be

- Prevent making a faux pas by contacting and involving the wrong person

- Find the most direct route to achieving your results

FORMAL STRUCTURES

There are different formal organisational structures, and it helps to know which one you're joining. You'll be most familiar with a traditional hierarchical structure, where each manager within the organisation has direct reports. But, this isn't always the case, and it's important to be clear on this from your first day on the job. You may find you're now employed by an organisation that has:

- A matrix structure - reporting to more than one person

- An organic or flat structure - with company-wide collaboration

- An advisory authority - like an HR department

- Virtual structures - which may stand alone or be in addition to another structure[1]

The beauty of formal networks such as these is that, by nature, they are more easily managed. They are also able to increase the value while lowering the cost of collaboration - which is, of course, essential to the running of an organisation[2].

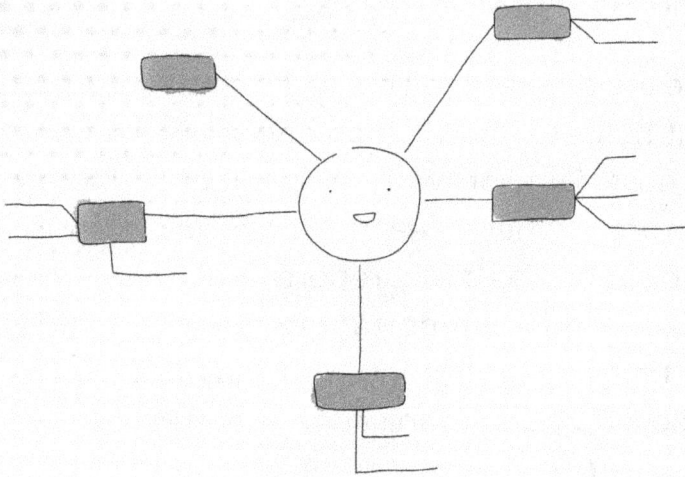

ACTION STEP

If you haven't already done so, you should obtain a copy of your new employer's organisational chart now.

INFORMAL STRUCTURES

Networks which have formed without the organisation dictating so, are known as informal. These are often built around shared interests and knowledge, creating an environment for the collaboration of ideas.

Interestingly, a study by Bryan, Matson and Weiss[3], found that the sheer quantity of information and knowledge flowing through these informal structures, far outweighs that communicated via official structures. In fact, they concluded that the "formal structures of companies, as manifested in their organisational charts, don't explain how most of their real day-to-day work gets done[4]."

Once you have a deeper understanding of the formal and informal structures at your new organisation, you're not necessarily in the clear. You may understand who to communicate with in certain situations, but you still need to figure out how to communicate via the right messages and signals. This leads you to a crucial aspect of onboarding, housed within the Structure aspect of the framework. That is cultural adaptation.

ALIGNING WITH A NEW CULTURE

In Chapter 2 "A Roadmap to Onboarding," I introduced you to a foundational element on onboarding: cultural transition. But, here, you're going to explore culture more deeply, by looking at the many elements of culture that govern organisational structures.

Have you ever questioned why something is done a certain way, only to hear the response "that's just the way we do things around here"? That's corporate culture, and, in fact, the McKinsey organisation coined this phrase[5]. And while it can be frustrating to hear, this is what you'll need to accept and align yourself with, if you are to succeed in your first three months.

Culture is what people do and say, informed by their underlying core values. Adapting to an unfamiliar business culture is often a daunting prospect for new employees and even those making the transition to a different unit within the same organisation. After all, culture in and of itself is intangible[6].

Once you understand the markers of culture, you need to look for how it shows up in the organisation or the subculture of the department you are joining. A number of models have been developed over the years to help people understand workplace culture and pinpoint its particular elements. When faced with the prospect of quickly understanding a new workplace culture, the Cultural Web by Gerry Johnson and Kevan Scholes proves helpful, as illustrated in figure 4-2[7].

Johnson and Scholes identified six interrelated elements of a workplace's cultural environment.

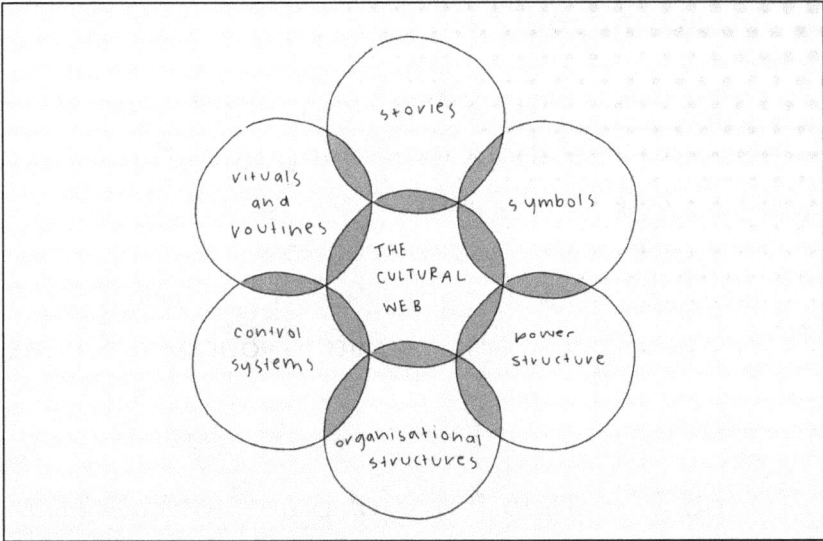

Figure 4-2: *Johnson and Scholes' Cultural Web: six elements of the workplace cultural environment*

1. Stories

These are the people or events that get talked about both inside and outside the company. What will tell you most about an organisation's culture concerning stories, is the repetition of particular narratives, often relating to the founding of the organisation. Stories tell us a great deal about the values embedded and then carried through the operations of the company.

2. Rituals and routines

These help customers and employees form expectations about everything from the service they receive, to how management handles mistakes in the workplace. Routines and rituals define acceptable behaviour and provide a guide for you to follow when auditing your own actions.

3. Symbols

Symbols include forms of brand identification, like logos, but can also show up as dress codes and the appearance of the office space. These are visual representations that give clues as to the beliefs shared within the organisation. While not visible, language is a symbol too and shows up in the use of jargon or industry-speak.

4. Organisational structure

You've already learned that organisations consist of both formal and informal structures in terms of official hierarchy, but also communication and influence networks.

5. Control systems

These are the controls that govern the organisation in order for it to operate effectively. Reward systems, quality assurance systems and even financial systems all fall under this umbrella.

6. Power structures

Rather than the hierarchical structure of an organisation, power structures refer to who really holds power and who gets the final say. This could vary from just one person, like the CEO, to a particular department. Strategic direction hinges on the say-so of these people.

STORIES

1. What narratives do customers, managers or employers tell about the organisation? These could be about the organisation's history or a portrayal of it now.

_____

_____

_____

_____

_____

_____

2. What do these narratives reveal about the beliefs held?

_____

_____

_____

_____

_____

_____

3. What do these narratives reveal about who is perceived as a hero or villain?

_____

_____

_____

_____

_____

_____

RITUALS AND ROUTINES

1. How do customers expect to be treated?

_____

_____

_____

_____

_____

_____

2. What are the commonly held expectations of employees?

_____

_____

_____

_____

_____

_____

3. What types of behaviour are clearly encouraged by the daily routines practised?

_____

_____

_____

_____

_____

_____

4. How is conflict handled?

_____

_____

_____

_____

_____

_____

SYMBOLS

1. Is jargon used and who uses it? Is it easy to comprehend?

_____

_____

_____

_____

_____

_____

2. What can outsiders perceive about the organisation, based on the visual representations like dress and branding?

_____

_____

_____

_____

_____

_____

ORGANISATIONAL STRUCTURE

1. How *do* people get support for their ideas and ventures? Via formal or informal channels?

_____

_____

_____

_____

_____

_____

2. What are the formal lines of authority as related to your new position?

_____

_____

_____

_____

_____

_____

CONTROL SYSTEMS

1. Can you identify control systems that work well and those that underperform?

_____

_____

_____

_____

_____

_____

2. How do reward systems function? Do employees value them?

_____

_____

_____

_____

_____

3. What reporting is in place to ensure control systems are being used appropriately?

_____
_____
_____
_____
_____
_____

POWER STRUCTURES

1. Who holds the power? Is the power valued or abused by them?

_____
_____
_____
_____
_____
_____

2. What are the key beliefs of those in power? Can you find alignment between your beliefs and theirs?

_____
_____
_____
_____
_____

THE CULTURAL TYPES

Another way to get a good grasp on the type of culture you're joining is to use Deal and Kennedy's Culture Types as a guide. Further to this, they developed a matrix that shows how the culture types are influenced by the risk in decision-making and the speed at which they learn if the decision made was the right one.

The four culture types identified by Deal and Kennedy and illustrated in figure 4-3 are[9]:

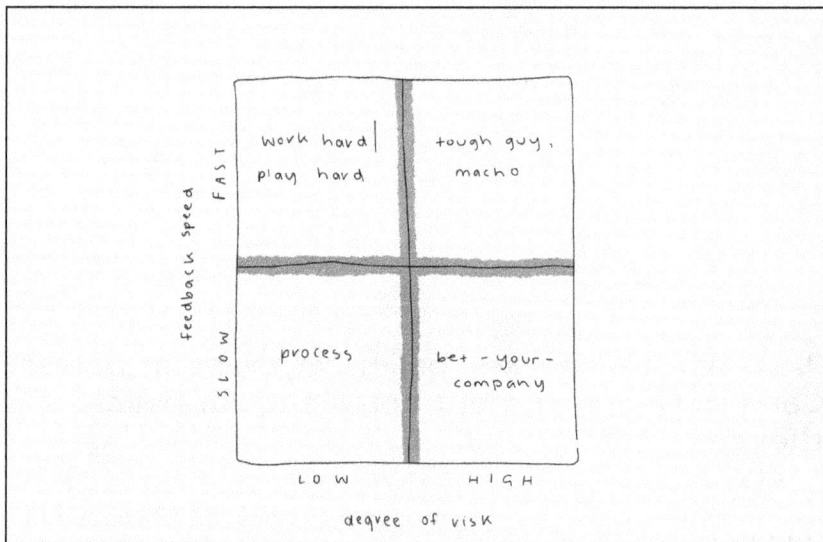

Figure 4-3: *Deal and Kennedy's four workplace culture types.*

Tough Guy, Macho

This culture is defined by individualism over teamwork. It's a "take no prisoners" environment with excitement and high-risk ruling day-to-day operations.

Work Hard/Play Hard

As embodied in the world of sales, employees aren't required to take many risks, but they receive performance feedback rapidly. Energy levels, a competitive spirit and yet an appreciation for teamwork are all valued here.

Bet-Your-Company

As the name suggests, the risk with decision-making runs high, but the company is playing the long game. A team-oriented environment is essential to making sure all the "I's" are dotted and the "T's" crossed.

Process

Low risk and slow feedback (as commonly embodied by government organisations) are characteristic of process-driven cultures. Processes and details are of the most value here.

ACTION STEPS

1. Can you see elements of one or more of these four culture types in the culture at your new organisation?

_____

_____

_____

_____

_____

_____

2. What aspects of these do you think you will enjoy? How can you align yourself with them in your first three months on the job?

_____

_____

_____

_____

_____

_____

DEVELOPING AND PRIORITISING VALUABLE RELATIONSHIPS

According to Harvard researchers Cross and Prusak[10], to increase the chances of you onboarding successfully, it's helpful for you to develop valuable relationships with a relatively small set of people. After all, when you need to make something happen directly, it always helps to have the right connections. I'm sure you'll agree that it's often not *what* you know, but *who* you know.

Without sounding too Machiavellian, the set of people you're looking for wear the unofficial hats of *Central Connectors* and *Information Brokers*. Cross and Prusak further suggest that you would make a mistake by investing in relationships with what they define as *Peripheral Players*.

It's easier to identify the people in these roles when you have a good grasp of the formal and informal structures of your new organisation. Let's take a look at some of the key characteristics of these people.

Central Connectors

The Connectors of an organisation are often larger in number than Information Brokers, and their amount of direct connections is also considerable[1]. Central Connectors are the people who frequently consulted with for their expertise and assistance with decision-making. They often take the roles of leaders, experts, old timers, gateways or political players.

Information Brokers

Information Brokers are people who leverage their ability to drive change, spread ideas or innovate. These people can also occupy liaison or cross-process roles (which link others who have information or resources). In other words, they bridge relationships between network subgroups[12]. Information Brokers may also be the employer's up-and-coming people who are helping transformational efforts succeed.

According to Cross, Paris and Weiss[13], interactions with Information Brokers are often "the most efficient means of gathering and disseminating information in a high-touch way. "

The good news is that both Central Connectors and Information Brokers are relatively easy to spot and often open to providing help. They are well worth connecting with.

Peripheral Players

Finally, there are Peripheral Players, who are less connected or may be less interested in helping you with access to information resources.

As a newcomer to the organisation, you are likely to begin as a Peripheral Player yourself, thanks to having few network connections when you commence work. But, developing strong relationships via purposeful networking is crucial to success - no matter your position in the organisation's formal structures.

Time is always pressing in the workplace, and never more so than while you're onboarding - taking on large quantities of information and developing much-needed relationships. I suggest you cultivate relationships with all people, but for greatest success aim to spend at least 80% of your time developing relationships with Central Connectors and Information Brokers.

ACTION STEPS

1. Identify your employer's Central Connectors

_____
_____
_____
_____
_____
_____

2. Identify your employer's Information Brokers

_____
_____
_____
_____
_____
_____

ASSIMILATING WITH STAKEHOLDERS

There is also the need for you to meet a range of people both inside and outside the business who are impacted by the projects you will be working on.

You can expect your new employer to provide you with a list of point of contacts for whom you can direct questions. Be sure to make the most of this and work out with your manager how you can meet with your key stakeholders. These are the people with whom you need to be invested in, for your onboarding success.

Ensure you're not only introduced to key stakeolders internally but externally too. They might be people who control information; suppliers and customers; cross-hierarchy, cross-function, cross-region.

Find out who these people are. Map them out. Over time, meet them all and ask them insightful questions about what's important to them. You'll find you can add to the initial list your employer provided you, as you become better acquainted with those who are crucial to your success.

ACTION STEPS

1. Key stakeholders internally

_____

_____

_____

_____

_____

_____

What's important to each of them?

_____
_____
_____
_____
_____
_____

2. Key Stakeholders externally

_____
_____
_____
_____
_____
_____

What's important to each of them?

_____
_____
_____
_____
_____
_____

3. Who controls information?

_____
_____
_____
_____
_____
_____

What's important to each of them?

_____
_____
_____
_____
_____
_____

4. Who are the main suppliers and customers you must deliver through?

_____
_____
_____
_____
_____
_____

What's important to each of them?

_____

_____

_____

_____

_____

_____

ASSIMILATE WITH SUBTLE NETWORKS

Subtle networks are informal, in that you wouldn't expect them to show up on any organisational chart. In fact, although these networks consist of members of your new company, they have likely been formed outside of the organisation.

Yet, as you've already discovered about informal structures, they account for seemingly inexplicable information flows.

These flows happen in a range of settings such as on the bus or train; or on the tennis court or the golf course; or during school or church events.

Subtle networks exist. The faster you can tap into some of them, the sooner you can get up to speed and successfully onboard.

Look out for subtle networks and see how you can join and make use of them.

KEY LESSONS

Before you proceed to the next chapter, I encourage you to revisit some of the key points from the chapter you just read, to help you master the formal and informal structures of your new organisation.

Remember: you want o show early on in your onboarding experience that you can deliver results.

But, you are not an island.

In fact, you are going to need all the help you can get. That's where networks come in.

An organisation consists of more obvious structures like formal reporting lines, but also a hidden network of informal structures that control the flow of information and influence.

Once you're clear on the structures, understanding how the six elements of culture are manifested will guide you in making deep inroads to these networks.

The six elements to consider are:

(1) Stories

(2) Rituals and routines

(3) Symbols

(4) Organisational structure

(5) Control systems

(6) Power structures

Adapting to these aspects of the business culture helps you cultivate relationships with whomever you choose, but I suggest prioritising connections with these key players:

- Central Connectors; such as leaders, experts and old-timers

- Information Brokers; those in liaison or cross-process roles and up-and-comers

Doing so will ensure you can tap into the information and influence that you need to make gains in the workplace, so you fit in with your peers and impress your employer too.

Chapter 5 brings the third alignment choice within the framework, from the subjective aspect: Style.

CHAPTER 5

STYLE

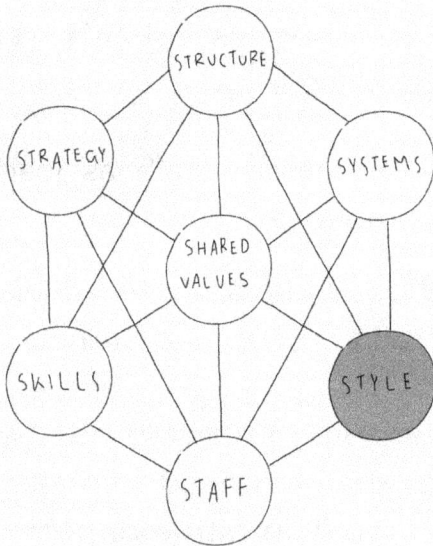

Just like Shared Values, Style is subjective, so has no hard and fast rules. However, by following some guidelines you can understand how to best align your style throughout the onboarding process.

Style is, in effect, your personal brand. In fact, the term 'personal brand' was coined by Tom Peters, the same McKinsey business consultant who devised the 7-S model. It was published in an article[1] for Fast Company magazine back in 1997 and asserted that in the same way that companies such as Mercedes, VW, Apple and Google are marketed as brands, people and their careers should be developed and presented as brands as well.

With the right style, you can build your own powerful and authentic personal brand. But it must be based on your unique skills, knowledge, experience and values as well as how you work with and serve others.

Therefore, your alignment choice for this chapter is:

- **To manage your personal brand**

MASTERING REPUTATION MANAGEMENT

Jeff Bezos of Amazon once said "your brand is what people say about you when you are not in the room." For a newly transitioning employee, you must ensure that whatever people say about you, when **you** are not in the room during those first three months, is **overwhelmingly positive**.

Reputation management requires the fulfilment of twelve tasks. And what is paramount, is how you prioritise among these to suit your situation. According to Peter M. Sandman[2], the tasks are:

1. Try to get people who love you a lot now to love you even more.

2. Try to keep people who love you a lot now from loving you less.

3. Try to get people who love you a little now to love you more.

4. Try to keep people who love you a little now from stopping.

5. Try to get people who neither love you nor hate you now to love you a little.

6. Try to get people who both love you a little and hate you a little now to love you more.

7. Try to get people who both love you a little and hate you a little now to stop hating you.

8. Try to keep people who neither love you nor hate you now from hating you a little.

9. Try to get people who hate you a little now to hate you less.

10. Try to keep people who hate you a little now from hating you more.

11. Try to get people who hate you a lot now to hate you less.

12. Try to keep people who hate you a lot now from hating you even more.

So, let's look at a few examples of how you could apply these.

Example 1: Try to get people who neither love you nor hate you now to love you a little.

When you're transitioning into a new role, with a new employer, it's likely that most of your colleagues will be strangers or little known to you. Therefore, the fifth task should be your highest priority - finding ways for those who currently have neutral feelings about you to love you a little.

Example 2: Try to get people who love you a little now to love you more.

If you did a great job of winning your employer over in the interview process, they might already love you a little. In this case, you would aim to get them to love you more.

Example 3: Try to get people who hate you a little now to hate you less.

Of course, your manner of transition comes into play here too (as we discussed in Chapter 2). If you are replacing an icon, for example, it's possible your colleagues would begrudge your appointment. In this case and as undeserved as their feelings towards you might be, you may be faced with trying to keep those who already hate you a little, to hate you less.

It's a case of choosing the appropriate starting point and then continuously working to improve your reputation.

DISCOVERING YOUR *UNIQUE* PERSONAL BRAND

When Google faced off with Apple in the smartphone world, as tempting as it might have been, Google didn't ask, "How can we differentiate from Apple?"

Instead, my guess is that they thought: "How can we be more like us? How can we bring more of ourselves into the work that we do?"

One of the reasons it is hard to copy a truly excellent brand is because they have put so much of themselves into their work. It's in the brand and company DNA.

There is only one Gillette, one Lady Gaga, and one BMW. Each of these brands shows up uniquely by being more of who they are.

No leading brand became outstanding by trying to copy another.

People don't want another 'genuine imitation.' Instead, people want to relate to and experience 'you' and the meaning you bring to your work.

After all, there's no more authentic and real way to be different than to be exactly who you are.

MANAGING INITIAL IMPRESSIONS

It's human nature for your new co-workers to begin making judgements as soon as they meet you. This is unavoidable, but there are ways to manage those impressions.

According to Harvard Professor, Amy Cuddy[3], there are two significant factors that contribute to a person's perception of you; your warmth and your competence.

Warmth is important because you appear open to building trust with your new co-workers.

Competency is important because it helps you communicate power to those around you.

It's natural that you might make mistakes or errors in judgement during your first three months, but finding ways to showcase your warmth and competence will stand you in good stead for a successful transition.

ACTION STEPS

1. How can I develop reputational respect by being competent for the work I do?

_____

_____

_____

_____

_____

_____

2. How can I authentically project warmth?

_____

_____

_____

_____

_____

_____

MAKING THE FIRST 6 SECONDS COUNT

I mentioned earlier that others will form judgements about you within just a few seconds. In fact, the first six seconds are the key to making positive first impressions.

And this counts even more acutely during your first three months. You are always under the spotlight, being evaluated at every possible moment.

Arguably one of the most famous pieces of research on first impressions is by Ambady and Rosenthal [4] (see figure 5-1). They found that:

By 6 seconds, people have formed an impression.

By 30 seconds, those impressions are locked in.

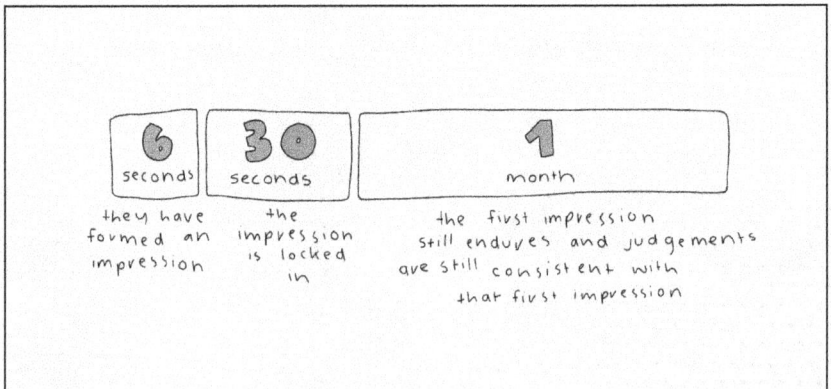

Figure 5-1: Ambady and Rosenthal found first impressions are formed in just 6 seconds.

So that we humans don't get into sensory overload, scientists have also suggested that the brain rapidly categorises stimuli or impressions into two piles[5]. For example: safe or unsafe; good or bad; boring or interesting, and so on.

Therefore, if you are going to form an excellent first impression with your new manager, co-workers and stakeholders, then you want to be positively classified by the brain from the very start.

If you do make a positive first impression, then your new manager, co-workers and stakeholders will be willing to engage more with you.

On the other hand, if you make a poor impression, they will switch off almost instantly. And once others are switched off to you, it could remain that way for months. A study by Gunaydin, Selcuk and Zayas[6] found that the perception of a person one month after making their first impression remained consistent with that first impression. One month after the first meeting!

So, back to Ambady and Rosenthal's research[7] which I first learned of when reading Malcolm Gladwell's *Blink*[8]. In this study, the researchers asked a control group of students to evaluate teachers with whom

they had spent an entire semester on a number of dimensions.

The researchers then showed short 30-second long videos of those same teachers to another group of students who had never been in a class taught by those same teachers.

What was amazing was that the second group of students only saw 30-second 'thin slices' of the videos of the teachers. Yet they made almost the same evaluations.

These so-called 'thin slices' were enough for evaluations (in other words first impressions) that closely mirrored the final evaluations by students who sat through an entire semester of lectures.

So if people make snap decisions on first impressions, then it probably comes as no surprise that bad first impressions are very hard to budge.

Take the phenomenon of a psychological principle called "fundamental attribution error". Once you are categorised as bad, boring or dishonest, then according to the psychological principle of fundamental attribution error alone, it takes an awful amount of effort to budge impressions and redefine someone's perception.

Now your mother might give you multiple chances. However, it is doubtful that anyone else will give you a second chance.

That's why the saying holds so much weight that "You only get one chance to make a positive first impression."

5 TIPS FOR CREATING POSITIVE FIRST IMPRESSIONS

As Will Rogers famously said, "You never get a second chance to make a good first impression."

To set things up positively from the start, here are several tips - all focused on helping you make the first few seconds of an interaction work **for** you, rather than **against** you.

1. Put a smile on the dial

Over the millennia, we humans have been pre-programmed to discern a genuine smile from a non-genuine one. The Duchenne smile is recognised as being natural as opposed to a false grin plonked on your face.

Before to going to meet anyone who might impact your success - especially in your first three months, it's helpful to think of a situation that made you genuinely happy in the past. This will bring out the Duchenne smile and subtly signal to the person you are meeting that you are an approachable, engaging and likeable person.

The aim is for people to spend the first few seconds thinking that you are warm and outgoing, confident, and professional. You can achieve much of this with a genuine smile.

> "Part of that is all those subtle signals that people pick up like are you standing upright enough, is your voice dominant enough, not too hesitant and not too submissive."
>
> **Andrew O'Keefe**
> *Author & Director*

2. No limp fish handshake (no bone crusher either)

There is nothing worse than having an awkward handshake. The 'limp fish' conveys the impression that you are a weak and unimpressive person. On the other hand, they might misconstrue a bone-crushing handshake as falsely dominating.

So, when you shake hands with anyone the first time, look at them confidently in the eyes, with a smile on your face, and ideally with both your hand and the other person's hand meeting in the same vertical position.

If your hand is above theirs, it creates an uncomfortable body language signal that you are trying to dominate them. A neutral handshake is in a vertical position.

3. Executive assistants rule

Many people forget how important an executive assistant is to their manager. But, executive assistants have been known to be asked by their manager what they think of a new person and what impression the new employee made on them.

To make sure you create positive impressions in your first three months, arrive a little earlier than needed, to allow you to freshen up and calm down. Compose yourself, visualise the meeting ahead, breathe out to calm any nerves, and engage with the manager's executive assistant in the same warm and friendly manner you will use with their manager.

4. **The eyes have it**

Body language experts say that people seem to be rude, nervous, shy or even untrustworthy if they don't make eye contact. Therefore, good eye contact is vital to creating good first impressions.

Especially in your first three months, make sure you are not just smiling and shaking hands confidently, but also looking the other person in the eyes while you introduce yourself. Try to hold the person's eyes initially and focus on their name - even repeating it in the next five seconds with " nice to meet you Amanda" is a worthwhile strategy.

5. **Dress smart and smartly**

Your organisation has its own dress style. So that you create a positive impression in the first few seconds, become aware very early in your employment on what the organisation values by way of a dress code. Even if the company allows casual dress, it's probably a smart idea to dress just a little smarter in your first three months, but not so much as to show that you are too different from the 'tribe' you are trying to fit in with.

A lot of this may seem obvious. But even the most seasoned employees create poor first impressions in their first meetings by breaching one or more of these points. Get ahead of the game, and make sure you master these five tips for a stellar first impression.

ACCUMULATING REPUTATIONAL CREDITS

Building a stock of 'reputational credits' is critical - especially if you are new to a role.

If you're in a position where you can consistently deliver on your promises, project confidence and meet and surpass expectations, then you will build a stock of 'reputational credits' and, as a result, increase your employer's trust in your abilities.

The process of building up reputational credits does not happen overnight, but the sooner this starts, the better.

The best ways to accumulate reputational credits are to:

1. Perform at your job

It goes without saying that it's essential for you to develop a consistent reputation in delivering well whatever is in your job description, almost from the get-go.

2. Work longer hours

This may sound dated, but it is the reality for most workplaces. Working longer hours is still often a prerequisite for making it through your first three months and beyond. There is no doubt that your willingness to work later and put in extended hours profoundly impacts your manager's perception.

3. Help your manager look good

The best way to make your manager look good is for you to perform at your job. You should also **only speak favourably** about your manager to any work colleagues.

It's important not to go to your manager with problems. Instead, give your manager ideas and suggestions. If you are helpful and help them to look good to their superiors, then your manager will be more motivated to support you.

4. Go the extra mile

Continually look for ways to over-deliver. You might consider offering to take on additional responsibilities and duties such as working back on a presentation or report. These are beneficial opportunities for you to highlight the quality of your work, build your personal brand and build reputational credits.

5. Widen your relationships

Whether it's working with people from other departments on projects, having drinks after work or making an effort to catch up with key colleagues for a coffee, it's great to network and build up connections that are wider than your immediate work group - especially with Central Connectors and Information Brokers as we discussed in Chapter 4.

Above all, seize any opportunity to work on a project with your manager, or their manager, which gives you further potential to build your reputational credits.

STYLE

5

ACTION STEPS

1. Perform at your job

What are the most important KPIs that you must deliver upon?

_____

_____

_____

_____

_____

_____

2. Work longer hours

If you were to work longer hours, on what projects related to performing to your most import KPIs would you be willing to work?

_____

_____

_____

_____

_____

_____

3. Help your manager to look good

What solutions can you offer that present currently as issues/problems in delivering to your KPIs?

_____

_____

_____

_____

_____

_____

4. Go the extra mile

What ways can you over-deliver in your role?

_____

_____

_____

_____

_____

_____

5. Widen your relationships

Which Central Connectors and Information Brokers do you need to connect with to deliver on your KPIs optimally?

_____

_____

_____

_____

_____

_____

What's important to each of the Central Connectors and Information Brokers?

_____

_____

_____

_____

_____

_____

CRAFTING A COMPELLING ELEVATOR STATEMENT

When you start in a new role, it helps to be able to explain to others what you do. An elevator statement or pitch is a concise, well-rehearsed summary of your value proposition. Metaphorically, we all know an elevator statement or pitch should be delivered in 30 to 90 seconds - the time it takes an elevator to ride from the ground floor to the top floor.

If you are not comfortable with the elevator analogy, another way to think about it is a 'BBQ Statement', or a 'Pub Pitch'. So, whether you're having a chat while cooking a steak at a BBQ or it's over a beer at the pub, this is about helping the recipient of your

pitch 'get you' in the first few seconds of their time with you.

The most common question that everybody gets asked at networking events and parties is, of course: "So, what do you do?"

Answers can be anywhere between the sizzlingly curious, to the utterly boring and long-winded. What you want to be is sizzlingly curious to the other person, while helping them understand what you do and what type of problems or issues you solve.

To effectively communicate an elevator statement, I suggest you use a formula that I originally saw in Allan Dib's book, 'The 1-Page Marketing Plan' [9]. I call it the PSP framework, which looks like this (see figure 5-2):

You know (Problem)? **P**
Well, what I do is (Solution). **S**
In fact (Proof). **P**

You always introduce the problem with "You know how ..."
You always introduce the solution with "Well what I do is ..."
You always provide proof with "In fact, ..."

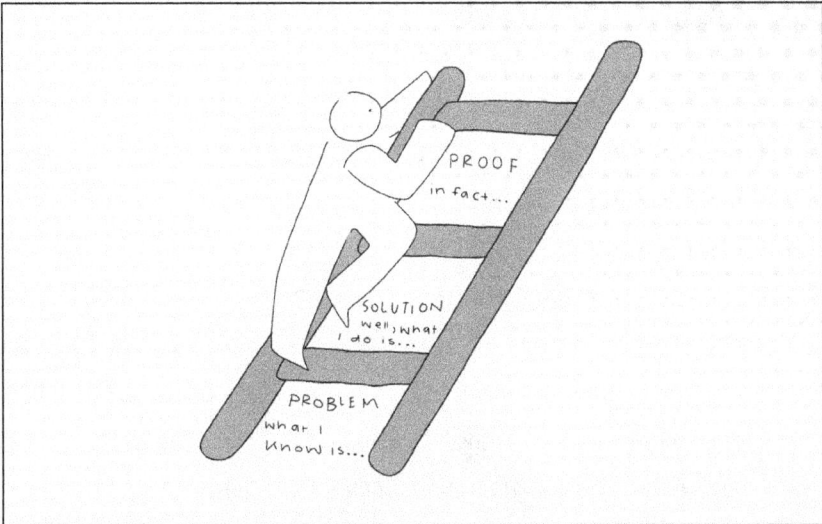

Figure 5-2: *The PSP framework for crafting an elevator statement, inspired by Allan Dib's formula.*

Here are three examples to guide you in developing your own elevator statement:

For a tax accountant:

You know how people pay too much income tax. Well, what I do is legally reduce tax for all my personal and corporate clients. In fact, I just reduced the income tax for a company that paid a $2 million tax bill the prior year to $1 million and for one personal client I was even able to get him a refund.

For a mortgage broker:

You know how most people finance their home and continue to pay that mortgage year-in, year-out without questioning that arrangement. Well, what I do is help people know what the latest mortgage offerings are in the market and how they could roll over from their existing provider to a better provider. In fact, just last week, a client of mine was able to reduce his annual mortgage repayments by over $7,000 by switching to the provider we recommended.

For a payroll manager:

You know how one of the most annoying and disengaging things any employer can do is incorrectly process employee's pay. It peeves the employee and ties up the employer's payroll department's resources. Well, what I do is to make sure every payroll run complies with all awards and contracts, consistently providing error-free processing. In fact, in the last year, I've been able to reduce the number of calls our Payroll Department receives from 100 complaints per payroll run to zero.

The PSP (Problem, Solution, Proof) Elevator Statement framework works better than most other frameworks I've encountered.

It's simple.
It's easy to understand.
It does not take a lot of effort to learn.

Now, it's over to you.

ACTION STEPS

Develop your own Elevator Statement for your new role

1. "You know (Problem)? **P**

_____
_____
_____
_____
_____

2. Well, what I do is (Solution). **S**

_____
_____
_____
_____
_____

3. In fact (Proof)." **P**

_____
_____
_____
_____
_____

KEY LESSONS

Before you proceed to the next chapter, I encourage you to revisit some of the key points from the chapter you just read, to help you manage your personal brand and create positive first impressions that position you for success.

Your personal brand should be unique to you, based on a culmination of your own skills, knowledge, experience, values and how you interact with others.

However, there are two primary aspects that are important to display, no matter what your personal brand:

- Warmth

- Competence

These factors will help you overcome the difficulty that first impressions are formed incredibly fast. To ensure you give your new coworkers a positive first impression, it's critical you make the first six seconds count.

Six seconds doesn't leave much room to get creative, but you can make the best of every one of those seconds by:

- Smiling genuinely
- Giving a firm, vertical handshake
- Making eye contact while introducing yourself
- Repeating their name
- Dressing appropriately

Once you have established positive impressions, it's time to start managing your reputation by building reputational credits through how you work and how you communicate with others.

And remember, whatever your reputation's starting point, you should always be working on taking it to the next level.

Chapter 6 brings your fourth alignment choice: to apply your strengths to your role.

CHAPTER 6

SKILLS

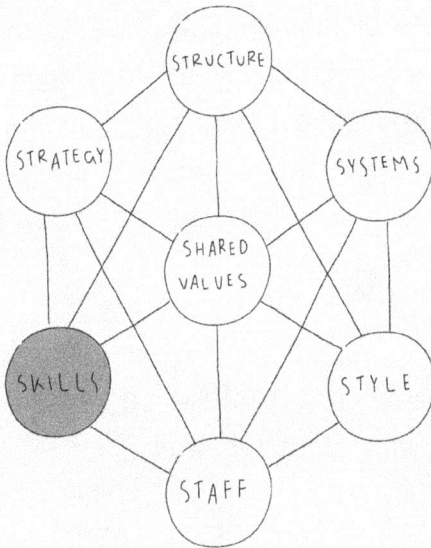

In a work context, Skills refer to the distinctive capabilities that you have and how those skillls can best be used to achieve career success. It is therefore a subjective aspect of the McKinsey 7-S framework and your onboarding process.

You have been hired into your new role primarily because of your technical skills or your perceived propensity to acquire those skills. In other words, your skills are your strengths.

So, what are your strengths? This is one of the most common questions asked in job interviews, and it's likely you were asked the very same in yours. You might have even had a great answer prepared in readiness, but, now that you've landed the position, it would be a mistake not to give it any further thought.

From your perspective of being new in a role, there are two crucial aspects of skills:

- Discovering which of your skills are of most value in your new workplace

- Matching and applying your skills within your position

What is critical is how you apply your unique strengths in those skills areas and at the same time minimise your weaknesses so that you successfully pass your first three months.

This is why your recommended fourth alignment choice is:

* **To apply your strengths to your role**

BENEFITS OF EXPLORING STRENGTHS FOR SUCCESSFUL ONBOARDING

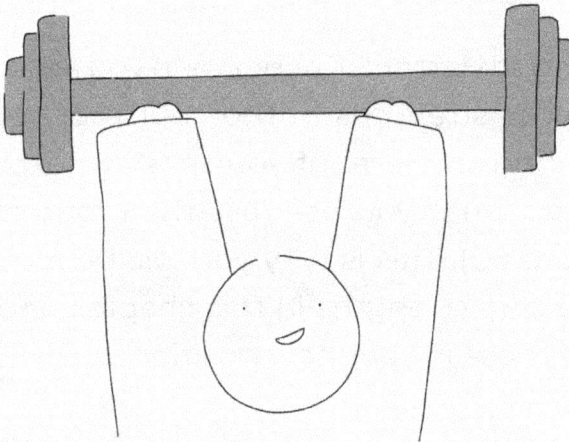

Like all of your alignment choices thus far, benefits show up at an individual level and an organisational level. One way to consider the two facets to these benefits is to consider the outcomes for a strengths-

based career and a strengths-based organisation.

A strengths-based career

The goal of this alignment choice is to discover how to apply your strengths to your new role so you may find professional fulfilment, but also success for you as an individual. In fact, based on a 3-year thematic analysis by Shane Crabb [1], 'Focusing Strengths' is one of three drivers at an individual level that foster employee engagement. These drivers create the internalised mindsets and attitudes necessary to achieve this.

According to Harzer & Ruch , when you apply at least four of your strengths in the course of your work, you will find the level of your positive experiences is higher than if you use less than four strengths (see figure 6-1). This is why you will be focusing on your five core strengths in this chapter, and how to cultivate these in your new position.

When you do this, you can expect to experience an increase in:

- Job satisfaction

- Pleasure

- Engagement

- Meaning

- A sense of power over your career

- Confidence and clarity around your value

- The vocabulary to articulate your value in the workplace

- Your understanding of how you stand out - as part of your personal brand

- Your appreciation for the value of your new colleagues

- And lastly, the likelihood of your surviving probation

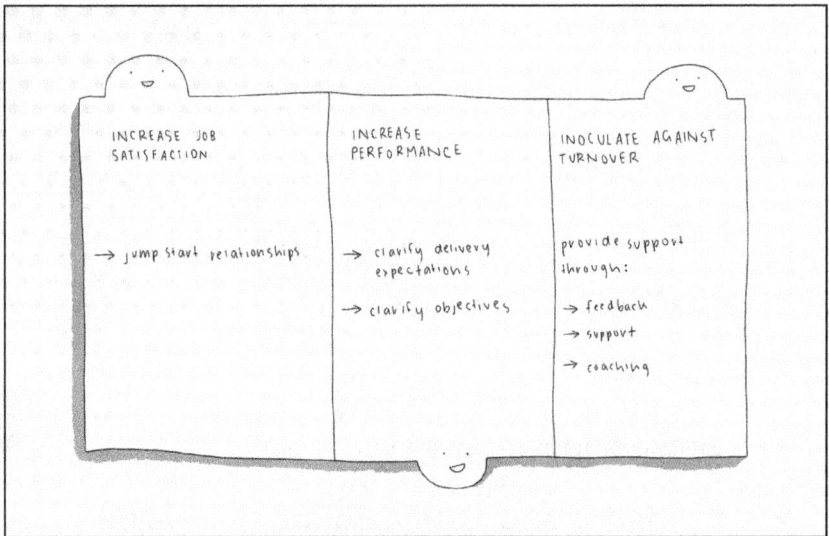

Figure 6-1: *The benefits of applying at least four strengths at work.*

You are in desperate need of strengths in your life and career, for your brain is naturally wired to favour the negative over the positive[3]. Actively seeking out and applying your strengths will help to provide a counterbalance to any negative feelings like doubt and insecurity as you onboard.

A strengths-based organisation

When employees and leaders take a strengths-based approach to work, it's not just the individuals who benefit, but the organisation as a whole. According to Gallup's research[4], the measurable outcomes include increases in:

154

- Customer engagement
- Sales
- Profits
- Employee engagement

Consistent with these outcomes is a decrease in safety incidents and employee turnover. These all add up to one thing: a more habitable and enjoyable working environment for you.

STRATEGIES FOR FINDING YOUR STRENGTHS

What are strengths exactly? Your strengths are what you are naturally good at and able to do consistently and predictably. So, they begin as innate but can be honed and shaped by the environment and of course, your actions. They tend to bring you enjoyment and fulfilment when you get to exercise them. But they also help you achieve peak performance results, which of course, benefit the organisation, as well as your career potential [5].

Some people are naturally aware of their own strengths, but for most people, identifying strengths take further consideration. After all, constructive

self-analysis doesn't always come easy! Therefore, I'm going to step you through two strategies for pinpointing your strengths before you match them to your workplace.

1. Take a strength-finding survey

There are several well-known strengths-finding surveys that you can access online.

A free resource that I recommend is the VIA (Values in Action) Signature Strengths Survey, which has been taken by over six million people so far, and devised by Drs. Neal Mayerson and Martin Seligman.

"Signature Strengths" refers to those character strengths that are most essential to who we are. Uncovering your VIA Signature Strengths can prove useful in addressing a range of life challenges, from the personal through to the professional. Therefore, this survey is ideal for the challenge facing you right now: your career transition.

ACTION STEPS

1 Register an account online at *http://www. viacharacter.org/Survey/Account/Register*

2 Now, you will be directed to answer 120 questions about yourself.

3 Upon completing the 120 questions, you will receive a report which details 24 Signature Strengths from most dominant (no. 1) to least dominant (no. 24).

4 Take your first 10 most dominant signature strengths from the survey and rate yourself on how well you are using each in your career, on a scale of 1-10 (1 being not at all, and 10 being all the time). Any rating less than 8 is significant. Ask yourself the question of how you can bring more of these underutilised strengths to your work.

_____
_____
_____
_____
_____
_____

2. Discover your Kokorozashi

Several years ago, I met two Japanese Change Consultants who proposed that you should look for your 'Kokorozashi' – Japanese for 'your something special.' Your Kokorozashi is your natural strength at your deepest, spiritual essence. Clearly, to act from 'your something special,' you must come at something from a place where you understand what your strengths are.

If you're having trouble pinpointing your strengths, it can be fruitful to ask those who know you best. Close friends, your significant partner, current and former colleagues, people you play sport with, or even your past performance reviews can provide much-needed insight into your innate talents and skills.

ACTION STEPS

What do your former and current colleagues, close friends, significant partner, your performance reviews say are your core strengths?

_____

_____

_____

_____

_____

_____

APPLYING YOUR STRENGTHS

However you discover your strengths, the important thing is to use them in your career transition and especially in your first three months. According to Morgan Roberts, Spreitzer, and Dutton, et al.[6] the aim is to get beyond the "good enough" to discover whether you are at the top of your game and progress your career. Here are five ways to get you there:

1. Find a role that allows you to exhibit your strengths optimally.

Although there is always a degree of freedom in the

execution of your role, if there is a fundamental rift between your strengths and your new position, this can only result in a world of hurt and disappointment. Ensure you will be able to use your strengths to their potential.

2. Make sure your new role uses your top 5 strengths.

This can be an excellent time to revisit the **expectations alignment** that you realised in Chapter 2. When your expectations of the role are clear, and you know your top strengths, you can review them together to see how they fit.

3. Determine when you are able to use each strength in your new role.

Following on from your expectations, once you commence your new role you will be able to look for the specific opportunities that will allow you to play to your strengths. According to Morgan Roberts, Spreitzer, and Dutton, et al.[7] , "most jobs have degrees of freedom; the trick is operating within the constraints of your job to redesign work at the margins, allowing you to better play to your strengths."

Keep in mind that there are many ways you can use strengths. These might be associated with a particular type of project, a particular aspect of the job, how you interact in a team environment and how you spend your time. It's important to think about your role in its entirety. After all, strengths and how you play them are far different to simply undertaking tasks you are formally certified to do.

4. Consider how you can bring more of each strength into your role.

You can be proactive about bringing your strengths more significantly into your new role. Try putting your hand up for projects that could be a good fit, or proposing ideas that will allow you to use your most proficient skills. When these ideas are a good fit for your skills, the confidence you naturally project will help convince those around you that they should be given the green light.

5. Avoid a role where you need to use much of your weaknesses.

If your role caters more to your weaknesses than your strengths, this might not be the ideal choice for you. Here, you will be at risk of spending your time mitigating your shortcomings, rather than building on your strengths.

SKILLS

MOVING PAST OBSTACLES

Many of us have been taught that our main focus should be to improve our areas of weakness, via a SWOT analysis for example. But this is a mindset that only results in avoiding failure, not achieving excellence.

Marcus Buckingham[8] said, "Most people are more fascinated by who they are not and how to fix it, instead of who they are and how to leverage it." This is a mistake. Instead, you need to establish how to capitalise on your Kokorozashi. In fact, your greatest room for growth exists in your strengths, not your weaknesses. This is so contrary to the usual approach, but so critical to success that I feel it bears repeating.

Your strengths, not your weaknesses, are your greatest opportunity for growth.

But strengths don't exist in a vacuum. They are still subject to our tendency for negative thoughts.

Unfortunately, fear can sometimes be an obstacle to embracing your strengths and projecting your unique skills. In fact, Buckingham and Clifton cite four fears in building your strengths:

1. Fear of weaknesses

When the fear of your weaknesses clouds your confidence in your strengths, it can make it difficult to move forward. But, know this - when you cultivate your strengths, you give your weaknesses less influence over your success.

2. Fear of failure

Going after your strengths can leave you exposed and doesn't protect you from failure. And that fact can allow the persistent fear of failure to stand in your way and inhibit your progress. It's important to examine that fear and understand that if you let it get in the way, you are only holding yourself back.

3. Fear of being seen as egotistical

Cultivating your strengths can easily be mistaken for egotism. But, it's important to recognise that when you build yourself up in this way, you are not making claims of excellence - and that is what egotism is. Instead, you are recognising your potential and taking responsibility for the outcomes.

4. Fear of being seen as an imposter

Imposter Syndrome is the voice in your head that tells you, "who are you to be staking a claim that this is your strength - there isn't anything special about you". But know that these insecurities are normal, and should be moved past if you are to succeed in your new position.

ACTION STEPS

1. What projects and deliverables can you apply your unique strengths to, so that you pass your first three months?

_____

_____

_____

_____

_____

2. How can you minimise your weaknesses so that you can maximise your time and resources and successfully pass your first three months?

_____

_____

_____

_____

_____

KEY LESSONS

Before you proceed to the next chapter, I encourage you to revisit some of the key points from the chapter you just read, to help cultivate your strengths throughout your career transition.

Your skills, in the context of this onboarding framework, are your strengths: those things that come naturally to you and you can consistently perform well at.

When you make the alignment choice to apply your strengths to your role, you see many benefits at an individual level including job satisfaction, confidence in your value and a better understanding of what makes you unique. But, for your first three months, you can expect the most significant benefit to be surviving your probation and continuing in your new position.

Strengths can be difficult to pinpoint through introspection, so taking a strength-finding survey or asking those who know you best can be helpful strategies for gaining a more accurate understanding.

It's vital that you deal with any fears that show up

for you when it comes to embracing your strengths and also make sure you are aware of the best ways to apply your strengths in your new role.

Next, Chapter 7 brings your fifth alignment choice from the 7-S model: Strategy.

CHAPTER 7

STRATEGY

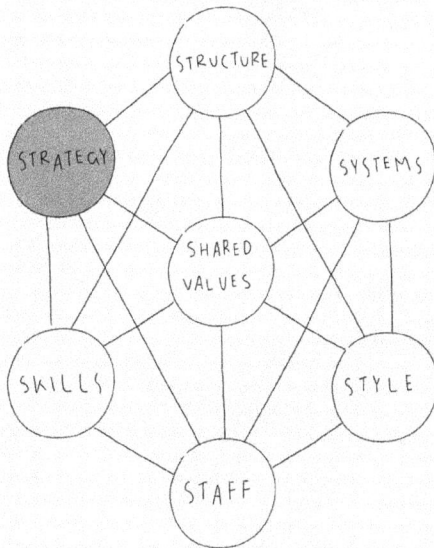

While most employees can explain their new role, up to 86% of employees can't articulate their employer's strategy[1]. And that's a big problem. If you can't succinctly describe the strategy, you could end up in one of these undesirable situations:

- Working on an initiative that gets knocked back because it's a poor fit for the strategy

- Being confused about the right market opportunities to pursue

- Being unclear about which customers are worth pursuing at all costs and which to let go

It's crucial to recognise that starting in a new role isn't only about focusing within your function, as many mistakenly believe. It's about figuring out how you can *provide value* in the context of the overall business strategy.

There's no doubt that this can be challenging. After all, you've been recruited primarily for one of two reasons:

- Your prior experience, including technical abilities, *and or*

- Your potential to be technically trained up to speed

It's easy to fall into the trap of thinking this is the extent of your function within the organisation. But, you're also facing a challenging situation where success depends on your capability to:

- Navigate the new business and political environment, *and or*

- Learn new skills

Therefore, the focus of this chapter is to facilitate you navigating these challenges successfully, by understanding your new organisation's strategy and adding value in this context.

Getting quick wins is the best way to do this.

This is why your recommended fifth alignment choice is:

- **To set up 1 or 2 winning projects**

IT'S WORTH UNDERSTANDING YOUR ORGANISATION'S STRATEGY

Even though leadership teams are responsible for developing strategy, employees at *all levels* have a duty to understand and execute the strategy to drive success.

According to Collis and Rukstad[2], the strategy lays out the competitive game plan for the company - in essence, what distinguishes it strategically. When you understand the business strategy, you can make individual choices that reinforce those of your fellow employees, thus aligning behaviour with the business for ultimate effectiveness.

You should learn to articulate the business strategy of your employer, or at least your business unit, using this framework (see figure 7-1)[3]:

- **Objective:** this is not the business's overall mission, but rather, the specific objective they hope to achieve. In other words, it is the 'ends'.

- **Scope:** this provides boundaries for the customer or the offering, geographic location and vertical integration, often defining where the strategy will **not** go. It is the 'domains'.

- **Advantage:** differentiating the company's competitive advantage is the most critical aspect of the strategy statement. It is the 'means'.

objective +
scope +
advantage

=

business strategy
statement

Figure 7-1: *The framework for articulating a business strategy.*

It's proven that those who have an understanding of the business strategy perform better, and as a result, move higher up in the organisation. Take the example of George Bodenheimer:

George Bodenheimer got in on ESPN in the network's infancy, starting just 16 months after the launch. His first jobs? In 1981, Bodenheimer worked in the mailroom and also in the administrative department. Over the years, he would go on to work his way up through the company, learning the business from the ground up, working in sales and marketing all over the United States. It would take him 17 years, but through hard work Bodenheimer would finally earn the position of Executive Chairman of ESPN Inc. in 2012, previously holding positions as president and co-chairman[4].

Like Bodenheimer, by understanding the business and its strategy, you will:

- Understand the priorities of the business

- Streamline your decision-making

- Align your daily **and** big picture activities with the organisation's strategy

- Have a clear direction

- Be on the same page as others in the organisation who focus on strategy, fostering better workplace connections

So, I've mentioned that strategy has ties to a business' priorities. And, according to Tom Bartman[1], a researcher for Harvard Business School, understanding an organisation's *priorities* is more important than understanding its capabilities.

Why is that? Well, priorities impose limits on the business, while simultaneously directing the business's focus. No matter the capabilities of an organisation (resources, staff and processes), success only comes from pursuing activities that are consistent with priorities and therefore, strategy. You see, if the business activities require additional capabilities to meet an opportunity, the organisation will simply invest in that capability. It does not work both ways.

ACTION STEPS

1. Ask those who are in leadership roles to articulate the strategy (ideally they will be providing similar responses).

_____

_____

_____

_____

_____

_____

2. Develop and articulate your own understanding of the organisation's current strategy.

_____

_____

_____

_____

_____

_____

3. Confer with your manager about your conclusions.

_____

_____

_____

_____

_____

_____

WHAT IS YOUR PART?

Now that you have a greater understanding of the organisation's strategy, it's time to figure out your part in it.

To become aligned with your new employer's broader strategic goals, you need to have "line of sight" (LOS) to their strategic objectives. In fact, this is a key role of leadership - to make sure all employees have a clear LOS, because this means everyone understands and can *describe how* their work is part of the larger vision and core strategies of the organisation.

This means you can understand the actions aligned with realising the strategy, to translate strategic goals into tangible results.

According to Boswell, Bingham and Colbin[6], some of the main principles underlying the development of LOS include:

- Employees being involved in the decision-making process, because "those doing the work are in the best position to provide suggestions and make decisions."

- By demonstrating noticeable alignment with the organisation's goals, employees may be given further opportunity to be involved in decision-making processes.

- LOS leads to better decisions, and therefore actions because employees are empowered.

Consequently, you can see how clear LOS to the organisation's core strategies gives you a better chance of success within the first three months, as you proceed in your new role and for your overall career trajectory.

CHOOSE 1 OR 2 WINNING PROJECTS

It's clear that there is much for you to learn as you commence a new role, and therefore your learning curve is steep. However, you are also facing a precarious experience curve.

Traditionally, the experience curve was used to explain the relationship between production quantity and the cost of production. In this context, it proves that as production output increases, the cost of production consistently decreases[7].

However, the experience curve also has an application for you, in your first three months. For, it determines that the more experienced you are in your job, the faster you are at what you do. In fact, what you traditionally know as the 'learning curve' informs the experience curve because people tend to learn by doing[8]. Permanent changes in your behaviour or learning arise by learning and therefore, gaining experience, through repetition (see figure 7-2).

While you face a steep learning and experience curve initially, the good news is that your skills are likely to develop rapidly. Much like if you were to take up golf, you'd find you quickly improve for a time, only to reach a point where your golf scores round off as you become competent and start progressing at a slower rate.

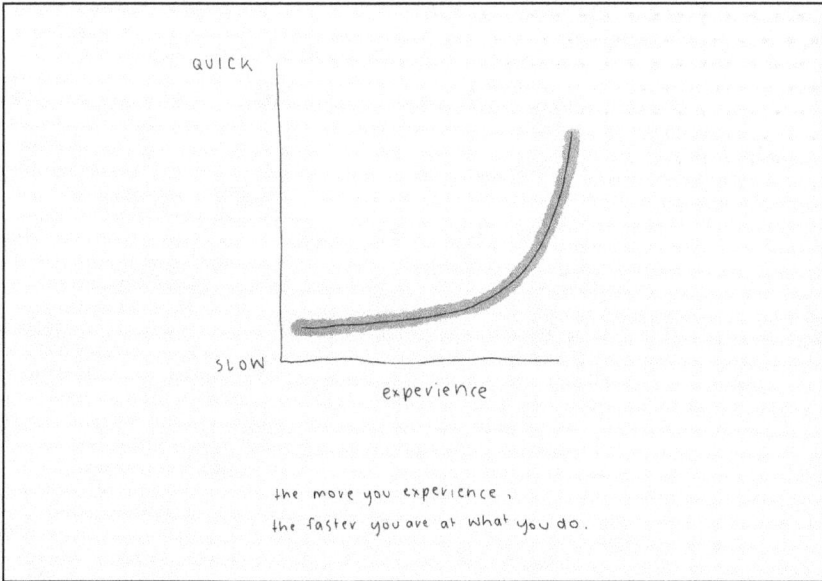

QUICK

SLOW

experience

the more you experience,
the faster you are at what you do.

Figure 7-2: *The experience curve dictates that gaining experience leads to speed in the workplace.*

As you navigate the specific functionality of your new role, as well as relationships, informal frameworks and systems, your goal is to get up the curve quickly to reach that point of competency. (More on this in Chapter 9 on Systems.)

Your best chance of putting this into practice is to focus on 1 or 2 winning projects in your first three months.

There are untold benefits to getting some early wins under your belt. Firstly, they get your manager excited. You see, your wins are their wins. Every success you have in your role reflects on them as your manager, not only in terms of achieving KPIs, but they are also seen as superior in their management of employees.

Secondly, early wins get your employer and stakeholders excited that you can deliver. In essence, your potential is realised - and fast. You'll have them thinking "if this is what you can achieve in your first three months, we can't wait to see what you can achieve beyond that".

One of the characteristics of quick wins that makes them so successful is the idea of 'ends'. According to Daniel Pink, author of *When*[9], endings are energising, elevating and have the power to shape how people behave. This is the reason why quick wins are such an effective strategy for proving yourself in those first three months. You see, when the end is in sight, you feel a goal is in easy reach (as in the case of a quick win), so the closer the end appears, the more energised you are and likely to see it through.

Keep in mind that the actions you take to get early wins, depend on your position.

If you are in a non-supervisory role:

Show your actions are in line with the culture of the organisation and what is important to your manager - especially how they are getting measured on your performance.

If you hold a managerial position:

If you are a manager of a team, you may want to model the patterns of behaviour you want to instil in your team.

When choosing your early winning projects, it's essential you find out where you can get the best leverage. After all, ideas are aplenty, but it's how you focus that will see you come out on top. One way of uncovering the best areas of leverage is to look at Critical Success Factors.

FOCUS ON YOUR CRITICAL SUCCESS FACTORS

It's easy to fall into the trap of being overwhelmed and being spread too thin in your first three months. To avoid these, I'd like you to consider the 80/20 or Pareto Principle. This principle represents the idea that most things in life are not distributed evenly[10].

It's been used to describe the distribution of wealth among the population or the relationship between customers and revenue, for example.

Another way of explaining the principle is to say that the minority of causes create the majority of effects. For instance, around 20% of your efforts, will actually achieve 80% of your results, illustrated in figure 7-3. The way to implement the principle for your benefit is to consider and then make decisions on how you allocate your time, resources and effort.

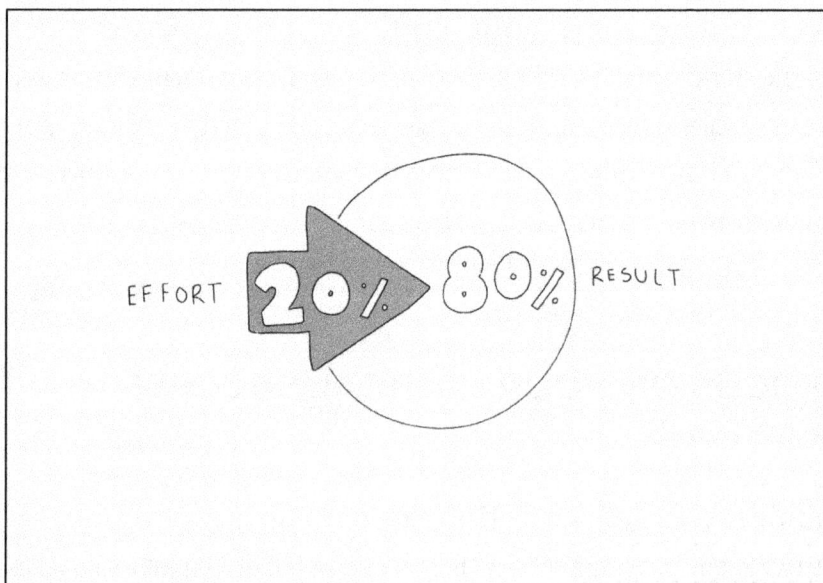

EFFORT 20% 80% RESULT

Figure 7-3: *The 80/20 or Pareto Principle.*

Your Critical Success Factors (CSFs) are those few things that, should you focus your time and effort on them, will yield the greatest results. That's why you should define and then take action on your CSFs using the 80/20 Principle.

CSFs are "the essential areas of activity that must be performed well if you are to achieve the mission, objectives or goals for your business or project."[11]

So, they are strongly related to your organisation's strategy (and your LOS), and these areas must do well for the business to flourish. However, they distil the business strategy down into precisely what must be achieved and how to do so.

Let's turn to an example of a Pharmaceutical Sales Rep, looking at his LOS and his KPIs which inform his CSFs.

The CEO of a Pharmaceutical Company wants to grow sales by 25% year on year. As a CEO, their LOS is the entire company and therefore larger than that of the employee who is a Sales Rep with a territory of say 100 doctors. The Sales Rep is only responsible for growing product sales in that area, and therefore

his LOS is just his territory, not that of the entire company.

The Sales Rep's LOS dictates they must only enhance sales in *their* territory of 100 doctors by 25% in line with the manager's goal.

His CSFs might look like this:

- Increase competitiveness vs. other pharmaceutical sales companies in the territory

- Attract new customers (not all 100 doctors in the area are customers right now)

- Sustain relationships with existing customers and incentivise more sales

When you compile your own list of CSFs, it might look much longer than this, and and that's alright. However, you should distil it down into five or fewer items that are *absolutely essential* to success.

When you've set your priorities appropriately, it's clear where you'll need to focus your efforts for the maximum results! According to Stephen Covey, author of the *7 Habits of Highly Effective People*[12], an effective self-manager knows how to prioritise important non-urgent tasks over urgent unimportant tasks. It is critical to identify where

your time is best spent and plan your schedule accordingly. If you want to make an impact fast and demonstrate your productivity to your new employer, this is the way to do it. It sounds easy, but we prefer to keep ourselves occupied, rather than doing what matters. After all, it's taxing to make progress, but it's worth it.

ACTION STEPS

1. What are your KPIs as you settle into your first three months?

_____

_____

_____

_____

_____

_____

2. How do your KPIs inform your CSFs? Be sure to narrow down to 5 or fewer CSFs.

_____

_____

_____

_____

_____

_____

3. What does your manager realistically expect you to deliver in your first three months?

_____

_____

_____

_____

_____

_____

4. How does your manager get measured on your own performance?

_____

_____

_____

_____

_____

_____

NAVIGATING THE POLITICAL ENVIRONMENT

No matter how well you focus on your winning projects and your CSFs, one thing that can quickly derail you is to get caught up in the political environment. Now, you might be thinking that you'd like to avoid office politics at all costs - we've all been there. But unfortunately, every office has

a political environment, and you need to have your own strategy for dealing with office politics appropriately, and to ensure it does not hinder your progress.

According to Karen Dillon[13], author of the HBR Guide to Office Politics, if you fail to consider how you will work alongside people who see the world differently to you, you will limit your career potential. You will stop yourself from growing, or others will stop asking you to grow. And of course, having this happen in your first three months could be even more disastrous.

Here are some key coping strategies[14] to help you navigate difficult political situations in your new environment:

- Remember that much of the frustrating behaviour you experience is not about you personally, but about their own inexperience, or possibly failings.

- You should find more ways to connect with people on a human level.

- Don't put all your eggs in one basket, by letting only one person (your manager) see your

performance. When you become part of the informal networks you explored in Chapter 4 on Structure, such as Central Connectors and Information Brokers, others will start to see you as three-dimensional, and they'll understand *how you add value* to the organisation, outside of your daily tasks. This helps to protect your reputation, by creating a sense of balance to any potential difficulties and should keep you in the running for future opportunities that you might otherwise have been passed over for. Network as much as possible to develop a foundation of trust that will support you in your new role.

- If you are hitting roadblocks with your superiors and must have a conversation about it, be sure to frame it in a way that explains how you want to do a better job *for and with* them and where possible, ask for help in achieving better results for you both.

- Finally, always check your perspective. Is there something in particular that you do/don't do that seems to trigger difficult situations with others? Some honest self-reflection goes a long way here and can often neutralise animosity before it gets out of hand.

ACTION STEPS

1. Work with your manager to find out the people who will be important for your success in your first 1 or 2 projects?

How will your manager connect you?

_____

_____

_____

_____

_____

_____

2. If you haven't already, ask your manager for a list of all the key people outside of your group who they think you should get to know, then set up meetings with them.

_____

_____

_____

_____

_____

_____

KEY LESSONS

Before you proceed to the next chapter, I encourage you to revisit some of the key points from the chapter you just read, to help you understand the strategy of your new organisation, as well as your part in it.

Recall that all employees have a responsibility to understand and execute their organisation's strategy to drive success. When you know the business strategy, you can make individual choices that align with it, which will help the business achieve greater results, but also help you cement your place and over time, move higher up in the organisation.

Aligning with your new firm's broader strategic goals requires a clear line of sight (LOS) and an understanding of your critical success factors (CSFs). Use these, along with your KPIs to work on one or two winning projects. These are key to your success in the first three months, as getting quick wins shows your employer that you can deliver and it excites them about your potential.

The actions you take to get those early wins, does depend on your position in the organisation. For instance:

If you are in a non-supervisory role:

You must perform in line with the organisation's culture and how your manager is getting measured on your performance.

If you hold a managerial position:

If you are a manager of a team, you may want to model the patterns of behaviour you want to instil in your team.

To avoid overwhelm while undertaking these initial projects, you should implement the 80/20 principle. Just 20% of your focused efforts, can yield 80% of your results.

And finally, remember to keep the coping strategies for navigating a political environment in mind if you want to ensure your winning projects stay on track.

Chapter 8 brings the sixth alignment choice within the framework, from the subjective aspect: Staff.

CHAPTER 8

STAFF

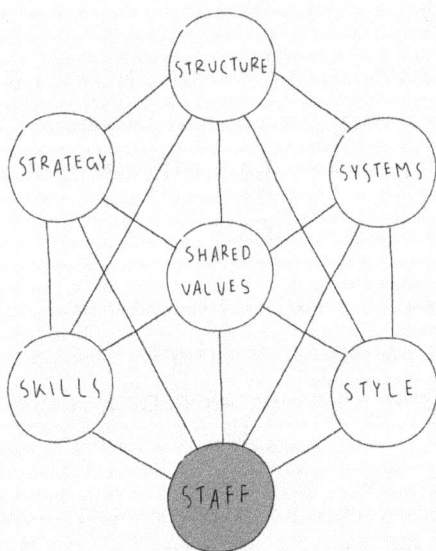

As a subjective aspect of the McKinsey 7-S framework, and therefore your onboarding process, Staff is where your people skills come into play. In Chapter 4, Structure, you learned to grasp the organisational structure including formal and informal and reporting lines. Staff is a deepening of these notions. In this chapter, you will pinpoint not just where your role fits within the organisation, but how you interact with those around you, to contribute to your onboarding success.

Therefore, your alignment choice for this chapter is:

- **To learn how to fit and where to contribute**

FITTING INTO TEAMS

Before diving in, I suggest you start with the basics to give you a better chance of success in this chapter.

So, what is a team? It's a collection of strangers that are united under a common goal who go through a process to reach a state of high performance. This takes time. Due to the uncertainty of group dynamics, a team is unlikely to be highly effective immediately.

When you start a new role, you can find yourself

joining any number of teams - from departments, to business units or as one of a group chosen to work on a particular project. As you onboard, it helps to understand how teams are formed so you can contribute appropriately from day one.

There are four stages of team formation, which psychologist Bruce Tuckman defined in 1965[1] and this model remains relevant for us today (see figure 8-1).

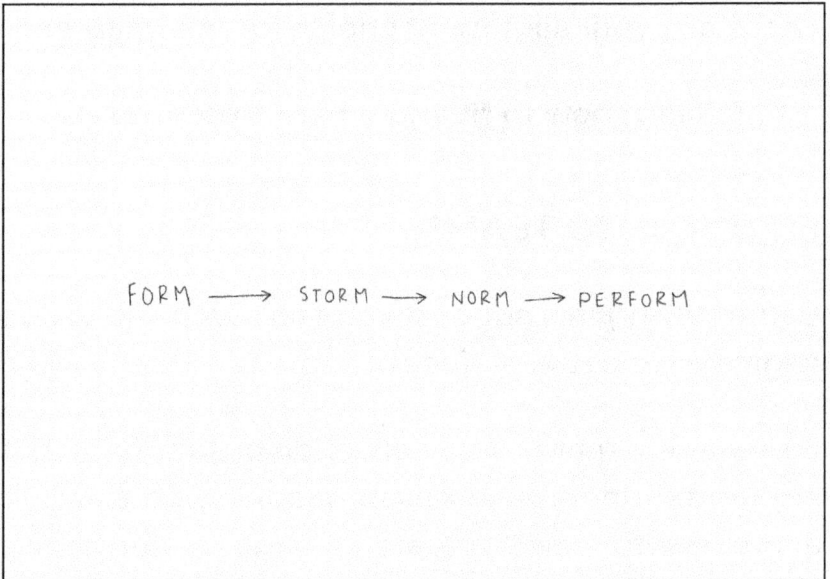

FORM ⟶ STORM ⟶ NORM ⟶ PERFORM

Figure 8-1: Bruce Tuckman's four stages of team formation.

1. Forming

In the initial stage, team members are usually polite, but anxious. Here, they are trying to get to know each other, so the team leader plays a dominant role, helping to define the responsibilities of each team member.

2. Storming

The second stage is 'make or break'. As the differences in team member's approaches or working styles become apparent, boundaries are tested, and conflict ensues. If some team members start to refuse to participate, there is undue pressure placed on the other members, and as a result, the team falters or even fails.

3. Norming

If team members continue to be actively involved, despite their differences, then they start working towards a resolution. Rather than getting weighed down by conflict, team members start embracing and building on each other's strengths. They respect the authority of their leader and strengthen their commitment to the team goal.

4. Performing

The final stage sees team goals achieved with hard work, but without conflict. The team leaders can start delegating more work to the team and working individually to develop each member's performance further.

According to Gina Abudi[2], effective teams share these common characteristics:

- Clear communication among all members

- Team member consensus

- Group brainstorming and problem-solving

- Commitment to each other **and** the project

- Positive and supportive working relationships

- Effective and inclusive team meetings

- Considered and timely handoffs between team members and stakeholders to keep the project moving

- Positive, supportive working relationships among all team members

You might recall that we talked in a previous chapter about observing chimp communities to provide a

greater understanding of what it takes to maintain organizational harmony. As Andrew O'Keefe, author of Hardwired Humans[3] has shown, we can learn much about team dynamics from primates. Baby chimps and gorillas are born with a tuft of hair around their bottom which signals to the adult primates that they are still learning the ropes of life and fitting in with their family group. Once their hair starts falling out, the leniency they were once granted starts to turn to discipline if they don't fall into line.

As a newcomer, you are just like a baby chimp. Your arrival can upset existing group dynamics if you don't learn where to fit - and fast. According to Tuckman, if the team you join is already at the performing stage, there's a chance you will not disrupt toverall performance. However, it's likely that - intentionally or not - your joining will see the team revert to the forming stage[4], causing the team to navigate through the stages once more. Of course, when you become part of a team, you should accept responsibility for any impact you may have and take steps to mitigate any conflict or disruption by finding out the team goals and roles and adopting them for yourself. One way you can do this is to ask to see the team charter.

TEAM CHARTER

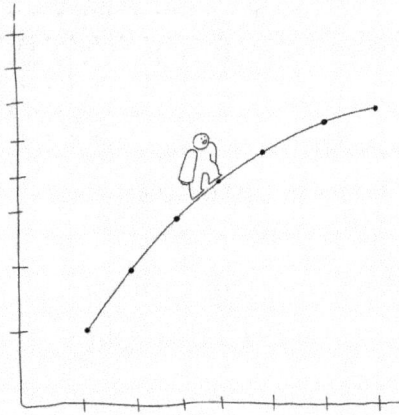

A team charter is a roadmap to define the team's purpose, processes and intended outcomes. It is ideally created in the 'forming' stage of team development so that it can lay a foundation for the overall functioning of the team. However, developing a team charter is also useful in times of crisis or when there are significant changes to a team. Therefore, if you join a team that does not have a charter in place, it's worth proposing this to your team leader.

Have you ever heard the saying "failing to plan is planning to fail?" This perfectly explains the necessity of a team charter to ensure the team's success. There are seven elements to a team charter[5]. Use

these to gain a deep understanding of a charter already in place or to assist in the creation of a new one.

1. Context

The charter must lay down the problem your team is solving as well as the intended result of rectifying the issue. It should also detail how this problem applies within the context of the broader organisation.

2. Mission and objectives

What mission must your team achieve? Define it using the SMART goal framework (*a refresher on SMART goals follows).

3. Composition and roles

It's critical that each team member understand where and how they are expected to contribute to the mission. Team members and their relative strengths should be matched to roles accordingly, with the responsibilities and intended outcomes for each person defined.

4. Authority and boundaries

Are there any limitations or boundaries to consider when team members are executing their duties? This could be in the form of establishing time constraints, a budget and an agreement of which decisions or tasks require prior approval.

5. Resources and support

In contrast to the previous element, the charter should establish what resources **are** available to team members. This may include training, coaching, people, equipment, time and budget.

6. Operations

This distils the 'big picture' mission into daily work. It can cover the specifics of team meetings, reporting structures and timeframes, as well as detailing the accepted method of communications.

7. Negotiation and agreement

In the spirit of teamwork, you can't expect just one person to be responsible for creating and managing the charter. It is a team effort that will require negotiation and possibly compromise, not only within the team, but with sponsors and stakeholders too.

Once an agreement has been reached, the team charter must be approved and committed to by all.

Abiding by a team charter will help you fit into your new team seamlessly and therefore heighten the chance of you surviving your first three months.

A SMART GOALS REFRESHER

It can be helpful to re-familiarise yourself with the SMART goal framework at this stage of your onboarding journey. Mindtools.com[6] defines SMART goals as:

- **S**pecific: Goals must have a clearly-defined target

- **M**easurable: For achievement of a goal to be recognisable, it must detail measurable timeframes, dates, amounts or figures.

- **A**ttainable: Goals must be possible to achieve (too lofty a goal will see you fall short)

- **R**ealistic: Goals should be sufficiently challenging, but not so difficult as to put you off

- **T**ime-bound: Completion dates and deadlines are vital

INDIVIDUAL GOAL SETTING

As well as following the goals of your team, you also need to have individual goals if you are to experience growth, professional development and enjoy a high level of job satisfaction. Just like in your team charter, you should also follow the SMART framework when setting individual goals. In fact, your new employer may require you to have individual goals if they subscribe to the Management by Objectives theory[7], whereby managers implement goal setting to:

- Boost individual achievement

- Improve organisational performance

- Increase organisational control

You will now have the chance to set a goal. But remember: it's critical that your individual goals should align with your team goals, organisational goals, and your manager's goals to support a unified purpose[8].

ACTION STEPS

1. With the assistance and agreement of your manager, determine an objective for yourself, applicable to your role, that also ties into a company objective.

Eg. Improve customer service ratings

_____

_____

_____

_____

_____

_____

2. Choose a performance goal that would help you achieve that objective

Eg. Improve the average customer service rating for customers you personally deal with, from 3.0 to 4.0, by adding a new touchpoint to the sales cycle.

_____

_____

_____

_____

_____

_____

3. Define the measurement you will use to track results and how often you will review them.

Eg. The organisation's existing customer service feedback metrics will be used and you will review figures weekly, at 12pm Friday.

_____

_____

_____

_____

_____

_____

4. **Is your goal attainable? What makes it so?**

Eg. You have noticed a disconnect in the sales process - the organisation is closing a sale and immediately requesting feedback. In your experience, there should be an additional touch point which asks if you can be of any further assistance, which provides the opportunity to resolve issues **before** feedback is given.

_____

_____

_____

_____

_____

_____

5. **Evaluate your goal. Does it strike a balance between being challenging and yet not too difficult?**

Eg. It is challenging because it will take more time to complete each sale in its entirety, yet all it will potentially take is one additional phone call or email per customer. You decide it is worth the expected result.

_____

_____

_____

_____

_____

6. Set a sensible deadline for your goal.

Eg. You set a deadline of three months to achieve your goal.

_____

_____

_____

_____

_____

_____

7. Seek your manager's approval before proceeding and then report back periodically with feedback.

_____

_____

_____

_____

_____

_____

BUILDING SUCCESSFUL RELATIONSHIPS

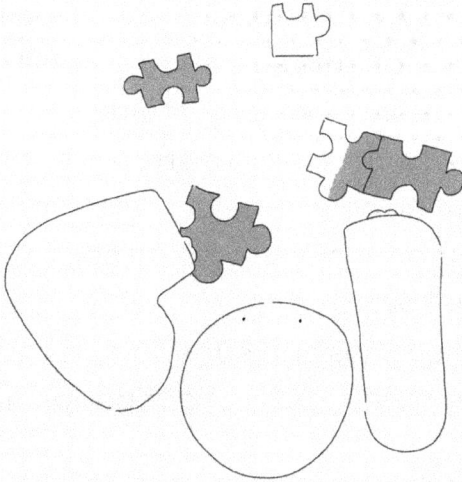

Just like your approach to onboarding on the whole, having a proactive attitude when it comes to finding your place in a team environment is critical. Following, you'll find some pointers for making new relationships more productive so you can find support to help you achieve those winning projects we discussed in Chapter 7 (Strategy) and generate some career-changing buzz once you've achieved them.

1. Find out what others need

In Chapter 7 (Strategy) you realised your responsibility for understanding and executing the organisation's strategy. But it's also your responsibility to develop constructive relationships. The best way to help others in the workplace is to leverage your own work to help them achieve their goals. In other words, find out what you can do for your new colleagues and superiors, in the context of how *they* get measured on *your* performance.

2. Ask for feedback

There's no need to wait for feedback - be proactive and ask for it periodically. If there's something you need to work harder on, you'll have the benefit of knowing now so you can achieve greater results in your first three months.

> "Gallup has been researching the engagement that people have with the workplace. It often comes down to engagement with your immediate supervisor, the person who you look up to. That level of engagement is the most important relationship in the workplace. That's a real move towards knowing who people are at a deeper level."
>
> **Robert Migliore**
> *Director of Actevate*

And, if it's overwhelmingly positive, you can reap the rewards of an interesting flow-on effect. You see, by receiving their positive feedback, you open a dialogue that brings your performance to the forefront of their minds. From here, it's likely they'll also be sharing this feedback with your manager. Of course, if your manager keeps hearing your name in a positive context that can only be great news for you and your career transition.

Even better, when your work makes life easier for those whose opinions matter most (like Information Brokers and Central Connectors) you're effectively reaping the rewards of both of these strategies at once.

It's also important to remember that at the heart of finding how to best contribute in your new role, is your ability to be assertive.

Let's start by establishing a scale, to make sure you clearly understand what assertiveness is. At one end lies passivity, and at the other, aggression. Assertiveness sits in the middle of these, providing the ideal balance for protecting your rights, without ignoring your employer's primary need of getting the job done (see figure 8-2).

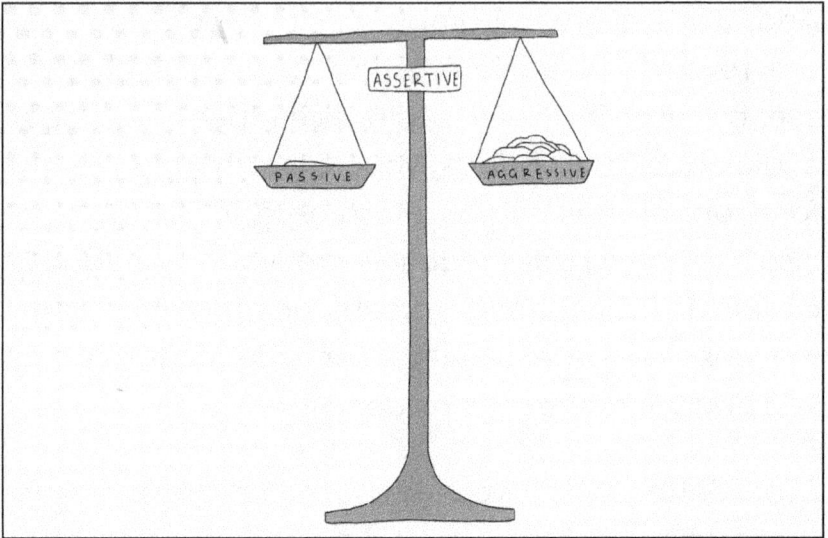

Figure 8-2: *Assertiveness is the mid-point balance between passivity and aggression.*

When you behave passively, you run the risk of not having your needs met or needing to compromise your values to do what others ask of you. When you act aggressively, you may come across as rude or hostile, promoting your own needs to the detriment of others.

According to leading chimpanzee researcher, Jane Goodall[9], "A real leader is one who leads because the others respect him and want to follow him." In her studies of wild chimps, Goodall found that alpha males who use a friendly approach hold a position of power for around ten years, while those who rely on force last only two years.

Whether you are in a leadership position or not, if you are to last in your own position, the same principle still applies. Using force at work is unlikely to get you what you want in the long-term. It's unlikely to help you gain the support of influencers, and it will undermine any power you already have. On the other hand, a passive approach won't see you gain any ground either. You will be seen as a peripheral player and it's likely you won't be invited to participate in upcoming initiatives. That's why an assertive approach, rather than an aggressive *or* a passive one is so critical.

Assertiveness is the sweet-spot where you[10]:

- Have a healthy value of yourself and your rights

- Can voice your needs confidently and positively

- Can openly accept criticism

- Know your limits and can say 'no'

- Use appropriate communication techniques to convey your meaning

Communication techniques you should employ include[11]:

- Using "I" in your assertions

- Expressing an understanding of how the other may feel or think

- Using emphatic and definitive verbs like 'will' and 'choose to'

- Be prepared in your assertions - this is particularly useful when you need to say 'no'

Assertiveness goes hand in hand with self-confidence, which can easily be shaken when you're starting a new role. That's why it's important to dedicate some time to assertiveness training.

ACTION STEPS

1. Identify whose opinions matter most to your manager. How can you develop your relationships in the context of doing your work in a way that makes their lives easier?

_____

_____

_____

_____

_____

2. How will you ask for feedback?

_____

_____

_____

_____

_____

3. How will you handle the feedback? Remember that being assertive (but not passive or aggressive) is critical.

_____

_____

_____

_____

_____

KEY LESSONS

Before you proceed to the next chapter, I encourage you to revisit some of the key points from the chapter you just read, to help you learn where you fit in a team context, and how you can contribute.

If you can gain a solid understanding of team formation and dynamics during onboarding, you'll find that you can intentionally cause less disruption to an already effective team. Remember those stages - forming, storming, norming and performing? If you can learn how to fit without the team needing to revert to the forming stage, you're off to an excellent start. You can also refer to the team charter to help guide you here.

Ultimately, you need to take responsibility for how you impact the team, but also for building relationships with those around you. If you are to succeed in your first three months and beyond, being proactive and assertive is a must-do.

Choose your individual goals, and negotiate for your own success, while keeping an eye out for misalignments.

Chapter 9 brings the seventh alignment choice within the framework, from the objective aspect: Systems.

CHAPTER 9

SYSTEMS

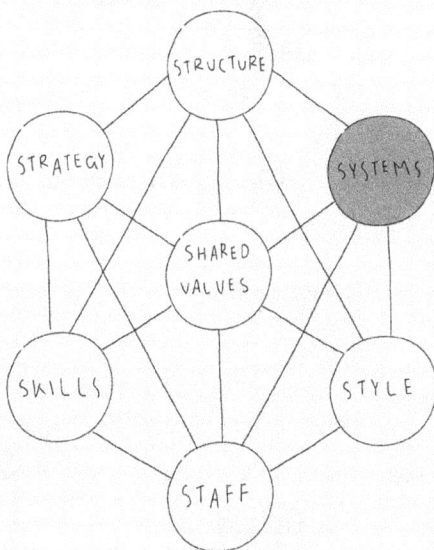

In your first three months, it is critical that you get up to speed quickly with the systems your employer uses. The systems that you find on the job might not be in line with your personal preferences. But, that doesn't matter.

Because what does matter in your first three months is that your employer expects you to fit in. You need to function and perform well, and as quickly as possible, using those systems. These include software platforms, email systems, phones, the intranet, CRM, all IT, the way meetings are recorded, task and project workflows, and more.

This is why your recommended seventh (and final) alignment choice is:

- **To learn how things work to support delivery**

It's been said that it takes 10,000 hours to master any one skill - this principle is representative of Malcolm Gladwell's 10,000-hour rule from his book Outliers[1]. But, without debating the merits of this controversial rule, one thing is clear. In your first 90 days, you do not have the luxury of finding 10,000 hours to learn how to use one, let alone many new systems. Luckily, there's a reasonable alternative.

Learn fast

In his book *The First 20 Hours*, Josh Kaufman[2] helps people understand that if you follow the right process, you can become proficient at any new skill in just under 20 hours, or 40 minutes every day for a month.

According to Kaufman, accelerated learning, or "rapid skill acquisition" does not require memorising the minutiae and it's important to approach it differently to academic learning. Instead, you should aim to immerse yourself in the central aspects so you can add that skill to your skillset permanently.

To put it in perspective, think for a moment about learned skills that you've been able to transfer (at least in part) from one job to the next. This is entirely different from the 'cramming' you did at school to just pass your exams - only to promptly forget most of what you'd learned.

Here's the thing. In your new job and especially in those first three months, no one expects you to be a world-class expert in one of their systems. Where it's at - if you are to impress your new employer - is to reach a *sufficient* level of skill for using *all* of their systems.

The 4 stages of competence

So, what does your psychological state look like as you develop the knowledge and skills needed to use an organisation's systems? A useful model here is Noel Burch's *4 Stages of Competence*[3], which was originally known as the *Four Stages for Learning Any New Skills* in the 1970s (see figure 9-1). It is a hierarchy of competence, that shows your starting point at the foundation, through to reaching a level of unconscious competence at its peak. Take a look:

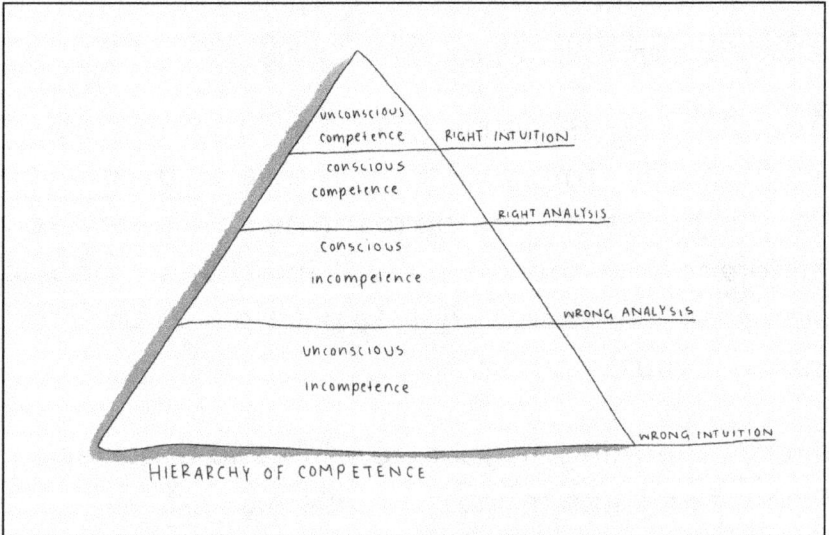

Figure 9-1: Noel Burch's 4 Stages of Competence.

Stage 1: Unconscious Incompetence
I don't know what I don't know

When you commence your role with your new employer, you might be oblivious to your incompetence - after all, you may not even be aware of the many systems that will soon come to form part of your daily working life. That's completely acceptable because as soon as you become aware of your ineptitude with each system, you can start to develop the skills you so sorely need.

Stage 2: Consciously Incompetent
I know what I don't know

In this stage, you become aware of your incompetencies or skill deficits. Perhaps you've been faced with a new system that you didn't realise your new employer uses, or a system that you assumed you know how to use, only to discover that this organisation uses that system in a completely different way to your previous employer.

It can be an uncomfortable feeling to realise your failings at using a system. But, if you are determined to learn, the only way from here is up. For at this stage, you recognise what the keys are to competency,

which gives you a direction and hope. As of now, you are considering the measures you should take to reach competency.

Stage 3: Consciously Competent
I grow and know, and it starts to show

It's time to dedicate yourself to learning what you need to know and to practise to reach permanent competence. This is the stage where you will follow Josh Kaufman's steps to accelerated learning, which you will read about shortly.

Stage 4: Unconsciously Competent
I simply go because of what I know

When you've reached the fourth stage, you're in the clear. You've done everything in your power to learn your employer's new systems and so you're able to use them with ease. Unlike while you were learning, you no longer need to think through each step or consult your notes. You simply do.

5 STEPS TO LEARN SOMETHING QUICKLY

According to Kaufman[4], these five steps will help you learn anything quickly.

1. Define what you want to learn

This includes your preferred "target performance level". Be specific and keep fine-tuning your goal until you know precisely what you want to learn and what that involves.

2. Break down the skill into its basic components

Most skills are not merely single skills. Instead, they are made up of a collection of sub-skills. Take the example of golf. Driving and putting are stand-alone skills with little in common, but both are essential to the game. Kaufman suggests fragmenting your goal into its most rudimentary parts, then focus on practising the most crucial sub-skills.

3. Identify the critical sub-skills involved in reaching your goal

Review 3 to 5 helpful resources such as manuals, videos or online tutorials. Browse through them to identify the tips that are common to all resources. Build an understanding of how to improve in those

areas. Practice those sub-skills first and repeat as often as you can.

4. Eliminate any obstacles to practising.

Eliminate all distractions so you can conduct focused, uninterrupted practice in peace. Make it easy to find and use the equipment, so you have no justification for not practising.

5. Commit to at least 20 hours of deliberate focused practice

Don't be concerned if at first you are low on the learning curve and perform poorly. Put in a reasonable time commitment that will support you continuing rather than quitting.

There is research that suggests people advance fastest in the beginning when they lack skill. As you deliberately practise you will progress through three stages of learning:

- You will consciously think about every tiny detail of the skill

- Some skills will come to you more naturally with less effort

- Eventually, with repetition, new skills become instinctive

Your first 20 hours of practise will get you to a solid level of performance.

Often when a new employee flounders, failure to learn is a factor. There is so much new information to absorb that it is difficult to know where to focus and important signals can be missed.

If you *focus too heavily on technical skills*, it may be *to the detriment* of your learning about culture and politics.

ACTION STEPS

1. Define what you want to learn

_____

_____

_____

_____

_____

2. Break down the skill into its basic components

_____

_____

_____

_____

_____

3. Identify the sub-critical skills to reach your goal

_____

_____

_____

_____

_____

4. Eliminate obstacles to practising

_____

_____

_____

_____

_____

5. Commit to at least 20 hours of focused, deliberate practice

_____

_____

_____

_____

_____

ADOPT A GROWTH MINDSET

According to Carol Dweck, author of *Mindset*[5], a growth mindset is to have the belief that you can cultivate your basic qualities through effort.

It's essential to adopt a growth mindset in your first three months, as you will be more likely to invest the time and effort in learning. Why? Well, a growth mindset acknowledges that some of your aptitudes might not be where they need to be, but a fixed mindset says that if you don't have the skills now, you won't be able to learn them and you may as well give up. When it comes to learning in your new role, a fixed mindset is a form of self-sabotage.

I encourage you to take the action steps below and then spend some time reflecting on whether your mindset could use some adjustments.

ACTION STEPS

1. Do you avoid or embrace challenges?

_____
_____
_____
_____
_____

2. Do you give up easily or persist in the face of setbacks?

_____
_____
_____
_____
_____

3. Do you see effort as fruitless or the path to mastery?

_____
_____
_____
_____
_____

4. Do you ignore constructive criticism or learn from it?

_____

_____

_____

_____

_____

5. Do you feel threatened when others succeed or do you find it inspiring?

_____

_____

_____

_____

_____

6. If you answered yes to the first suggestion in each question, you lean towards a fixed mindset. Yes to the second suggestion in each question points to a growth mindset.

Where could your mindset improve?

_____

_____

_____

_____

_____

CONSIDER THE KAIZEN CONTINUAL LOOP

Along with adopting a growth mindset, what would your career look like if you decided not just to check off a list of the base level skills once you'd become competent at them, but instead, looked for ways to develop them further?

Imagine if, rather than just using the systems to the level you *must, instead you learned* to use them beyond that, in the ways your superiors or even other departments do. You could master the systems beyond what is merely expected of you, and showcase your potential to your employer.

This is called the Kaizen Continual Loop of Mastery, illustrated in figure 9-2. And while you shouldn't pressure yourself to complete this in your first three months, if you're learning quickly this could be a natural progression for you - and more importantly - a way to solidify yourself as competent and initiative-driven in the eyes of your employer.

Kaizen is the Japanese word for improvement. When used in business, The Kaizen Loop says that creating a culture of continuous improvement among all levels of employees will help them work in cooperation to build on the success of an organisation.

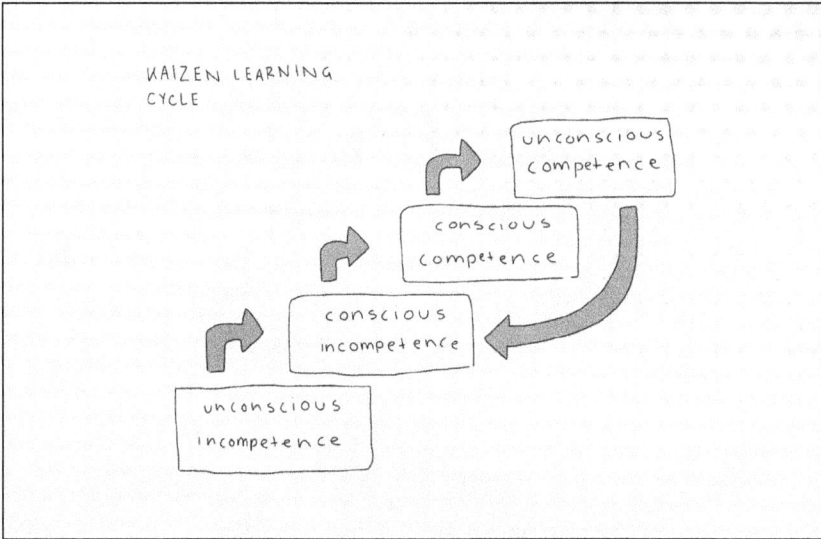

KAIZEN LEARNING CYCLE

unconscious competence

conscious competence

conscious incompetence

unconscious incompetence

Figure 9-2: *The Kaizen Continual Loop of Mastery for ongoing learning.*

But, you can use it too, as an individual way to build on your abilities and take them to greater heights. In the context of the four stages of competence, this means that once you have attained a level of unconscious competence, you determine a logical next step, which is ultimately a more challenging level of skill that you can use with a particular system.

At this point, you are reverting to the stage of conscious incompetence and then work on it once more until you are autonomous. This forms the continuous loop.

HOW DO YOU LEARN?

When you do start learning the systems your new role requires, you'll no doubt be learning from those around you. But, clouds can begin to form on the horizon when you realise that your learning styles clash. It's frustrating when you see they're investing time in you, but you just can't seem to grasp the concept.

Unless you can find a way to resolve this or work with learning styles that don't fit with your own preferences, you and your position at this organisation could be in trouble.

With that in mind, here's how you can avoid that happening and ensure you keep up with all the learning on offer.

Identify your learning style

I encourage you to consider the model developed by Dr Richard Felder and Barbara Solomon in the 1980s - *The Index of Learning Styles*[6]. According to this model, there are four dimensions of learning styles:

- **Sensory / Intuitive**

Sensory learners look for the facts and learn best from concrete or practical information. On the other hand, intuitive learners can learn more from concepts and theories. In other words, they prefer to understand the meaning behind something.

- **Visual / Verbal**

Visual learners prefer information presented visually, whether in actual pictures or as graphical representations. Conversely, verbal learners require words as the foundation of their learning. That means reading or hearing information is key.

- **Active / Reflective**

Active learners are great at teamwork because they like to learn by trying. On the other hand, reflective learners prefer to figure out problems themselves by analysing and weighing up the options.

- **Sequential / Global**

Sequential learners must have the smaller details presented in an orderly fashion before they can see the big picture. Whereas, global learners have a holistic approach, seeing the big picture before they are concerned with the finer details.

Evolve beyond your learning preferences

Your aim is to develop a more balanced approach to learning. So, by looking at where your existing preferences lie, you can see where you should develop beyond that. When you have a balanced learning approach, you can understand new information quickly and accurately.

It's easy to have a fixed mindset and decide you can only learn in one way. But, that will be a significant hindrance to you in your career. As you navigate the systems of your new employer, remember to be open to different learning styles, stay calm and, of course, ask questions.

ACTION STEPS

1. Take a moment for self-reflection and identify your own learning style in each of the four dimensions.

_____

_____

_____

_____

_____

2. Determine where you could benefit from a more balanced learning approach. Eg. If you're a strict verbal learner, you would need to attempt a visual learning approach.

_____

_____

_____

_____

_____

3. Establish ways you can learn with a more balanced approach. Eg. Rather than reading a manual, watch audio-visual presentations.

_____

_____

_____

_____

_____

KEY LESSONS

Before you proceed to the next chapter, I encourage you to revisit some of the key points from the chapter you just read, to prepare you for learning the systems at your new organisation.

Recall that you need not find 10,000 hours to master these new systems. Instead, just 20 hours of deliberate learning and practise will get you to the level of proficiency you require.

With just 40 minutes each day for one month, you can progress through the four stages of competence, accelerating your learning, so you become unconsciously competent. When you *simply go because you know*, you no longer need to think through each step, freeing up your time and attention for the most important aspects of your role. You'll achieve this (to your own and your employer's delight) following these five steps:

1. Define what you want to learn

2. Break down the skill into its basic components

3. Identify the sub-critical skills to reach your goal

4. Eliminate obstacles to practising

5. Commit to at least 20 hours of focused, deliberate practice

From an early stage in your first three months, it's helpful to define your learning agenda. You can do this in your first week, or even before you commence your new position.

To define your learning agenda, you must establish your learning priorities, which for now, are geared towards your KPIs and chosen winning projects. And remember to be open to learning in ways that may not be your first preference. Balance is the key to helping you grow.

Congratulations! You've now made the seven alignment choices necessary to become successful during the first three months of your new position. But before you go, I'll prepare you with some tools to help you face your first review with your new employer, with confidence.

CHAPTER 10

PREPARE FOR REVIEW

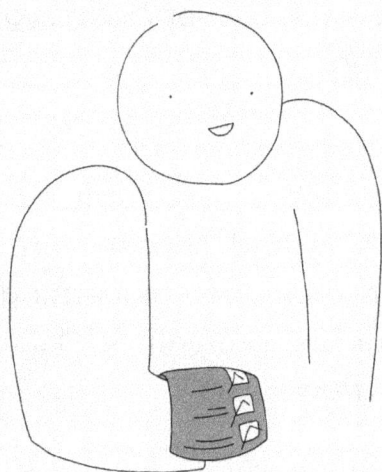

When you've navigated through the alignment choices and your first three months, you come to a pivotal moment in your time with your new employer - your probationary review. Much like when you commence in this role, you may feel daunted by the next step lying ahead of you. But, like onboarding, the more prepared you are, the better you can position yourself for success.

I recommend you start preparing about two weeks before your review. Keep in mind that a review is a two-way street. While the review is of course in place for your employer to share their thoughts on your early performance, it also gives you the opportunity to express your thoughts and ask for feedback that you feel you need, in order to do your job optimally.

With that in mind, you should consider preparing responses to questions your employer might have for you, but also your own questions for them. Here are the top strategies for success when it comes to sitting a probationary review.

STRATEGIES FOR SUCCESS

1. Prepare your responses

Your employer will be able to tell if you have given your responses some considered thought beforehand. It will also give you the chance to recall and then highlight your best moments. You can expect to be asked open-ended questions that will provide you with the opportunity to elaborate further than a simple yes or no.

2. Go in with a positive mindset

There will always be things you wish you could have handled differently in your role, but it's important to face your review with positivity. By having your successes firmly in mind, you will feel more settled and less nervous at your review.

3. Expect to be told what you can improve on

It's certainly nice to receive some praise, but according to Rob McGovern, founder of JobFox.com and Careerbuilder.com, focusing too much on praise is a mistake. After all, "unless you're dumb, you already know what you're good at" so you should "look at performance reviews as action plans - find out what you can do better."[1]

4. Be prepared to show an interest in your manager and the company

Surprise your manager. Don't make it all about you, but also about how you can contribute more to the company's success.

RESPONSES TO ARM YOURSELF WITH

You just learned it's important to prepare your responses. Here are some questions that you could be expected to answer, according to the 12 questions that Gallup researchers recommend employers ask[2]

1. Do you know what is expected of you at work?

2. Do you have the materials and equipment to do your work right?

3. At work, do you have the opportunity to do what you do best every day?

4. In the last seven days, have you received recognition or praise for doing good work?

5. Does your supervisor, or someone at work, seem to care about you as a person?

6. Is there someone at work who encourages your development?

7. At work, do your opinions seem to count?

8. Does the mission/purpose of your company make you feel your job is important?

9. Are your associates (fellow employees) committed to doing quality work?

10. Do you have a best friend at work?

11. In the last three months, has someone at work talked to you about your progress?

12. In the last three months, have you had opportunities to learn and grow?

Some other questions that may be helpful to think about here are:

1. Are you on track to achieve your goals for the first three months?

2. Do you feel your goals are still relevant?

3. How have your first 3 months been overall?

4. What would you like to achieve in your next 3 months, 6 months or even 12 months?

QUESTIONS TO CONSIDER ASKING YOUR EMPLOYER IN YOUR REVIEW

You learned that a helpful success strategy involves taking the initiative to show an interest in the company. Here are some questions you can ask that achieve that[3]:

1. What should I do differently next month/quarter/year?

Although you might anticipate your review will be focused on your past performance, it's important to find out how to move forward. Asking future-focused questions can take a negative and turn it into a constructive guide for the future.

2. How can I be more helpful to others on the team/ in my department?

As you've seen throughout this book, team dynamics and how you respond to them play a critical role in your success. Employers love team players, and getting someone else's opinion on how you interact with the team can be immensely helpful.

After all, there may be something you're unaware of doing/not doing, or there could be something your manager would really like help with but hasn't yet found the right person to task.

3. **What are your most important goals for next month/quarter/year?**

As the fourth strategy for success mentioned, it's vital to show an interest in how you can contribute more to your employer's success. Even though you might be clear on your own KPIs and goals, you should be aiming to understand and help achieve those of your employer.

Matthew Rothenberg, the editor-in-chief at TheLadders.com and co-author of *You're Better Than Your Job Search*, suggests drilling down further and asking[4] " what are the two most important factors that you want to improve in our organization over the next six to ten months?" and "what are the most important things we need to do to improve those two factors?"

Another question worth tying in here is to ask how you can make your manager's job easier. It's the ideal way to impress and set yourself apart.

4. What skills should I develop further in order to succeed in my role?

As you move forward, you will be expected to grow. Instead of wondering where you should concentrate your learning, why not just ask?

5. What career opportunities do you think there are for me here?

The single best way to show your commitment to the company is to demonstrate an interest in what your future career here could look like. Plus, it's a great idea to get on your manager's radar so they know you might be interested in new positions or promotions as they arise.

6. What challenges lie ahead for the company in the future?

Of course, if you really want to look like you're interested in the big picture, you want to find ways you can add value when it isn't smooth sailing.

EXPECT A WRITTEN RECORD

Employers often keep written records as evidence of reviews as well as the key points discussed[5]. You may be given a copy, and it will also be stored in your personnel file. If your employer does not usually do this - don't be afraid to request it.

Sometimes it can be difficult to remember everything that was discussed, especially when nervous. Having a written record will ensure you're clear on the things you might need to work on, going forward.

KEY LESSONS

Your probationary review is a pivotal moment, and you should treat it as such.

Remember to:

- Prepare responses to the questions you anticipate being asked

- Prepare questions for your manager to clarify your goals as you move forward

- Have a positive mindset, focusing on your successes

- Express an interest in your manager and your future at this organisation

You needn't feel like your employer has all the power here. So follow these guidelines, and you'll show up confident and ready to impress.

Good luck.

Chapter 11 brings us to the conclusion of our time together, for now.

CHAPTER 11

CONCLUSION

Congratulations! You've reached the final chapter of this book.

For now, I'd like you to pause a few moments and imagine what your career with this new employer could look like.

For instance, what would it mean to you if:

- You knew that you had the best preparation possible and are ready to face the challenges a new employer may throw at you?

- You felt confident in your place in the company and knew who to turn to for help?

- You could wake up each morning knowing you're heading to a job where your employer understands your value?

- You had ongoing stability with your finances and of course, your lifestyle?

- You could be assured you didn't have to step back onto that mouse wheel of sitting job interview after job interview for a long time to come?

We all know there is no such thing as a perfect job (although social media tries to tell us otherwise). But,

there are great jobs that you can be happy working in if you only give yourself a chance.

And that starts from day one.

HOW TO BE SET UP FOR SUCCESS

You might recall the startling statistic that up to 20% of employee turnover happens in the first 45 days, and that can be even higher for millennials[1]. That means you are at risk of not surviving your probation period and so you're cast back into the pool of the hopeful jobless, looking for your next great opportunity.

I'm sure you'll agree that doesn't sound like much fun, but the risk is very real. After all, that's why you're here, isn't it? To make sure you survive, and even better, thrive, in your career transition.

But if you want to succeed, you need to make a commitment to yourself - to stay for the long haul. When you embrace the challenge of a new position and continue to step up your game, it doesn't just help your career. It builds your confidence and identity in all aspects of life.

When given a structured onboarding experience, 69% of employees will stay on for a period of three years[2]. This is your structured onboarding program to guide you through the often murky waters of a career transition.

This book was designed to be a proactive tool, a reliable resource for you to apply in your first three months and beyond. I hope you use it as such.

I also suggest that the most important step you can take at this stage is to proactively seek out the support of your manager to give yourself the best chance of delivering to their expectations.

TAKE THE REINS

There's no doubt you're entering a period that is fraught with uncertainty. As a new employee, it's intense being under the spotlight and scrutiny of people who are essentially strangers to you. What can be even more daunting is that your manager has the authority to either make or influence final decisions on your employment status - whether that's just surviving the first three months, or making it long-term.

The good news is your manager and you both want the same thing - for you to succeed. But your manager also has KPIs which are, of course, their priority. Therefore, the best way to secure the support of your manager is to deliver to your *manager's* KPIs.

When you add value and help your manager look good, it's natural for them to warm to you and your work ethic fast.

If this is what you want - a successful and long-term career transition, then you must take 100% responsibility for your career. You can't expect anyone else to take care of your settling in *for* you. Your best chance of success and achieving job satisfaction lies in taking the reins for yourself to ensure you get to where you need to be.

That's why each aspect of the McKinsey 7-S model and the onboarding framework this book has focused on, relies on you *making an alignment choice for yourself* (see figure 11-1). Let's recap those choices now.

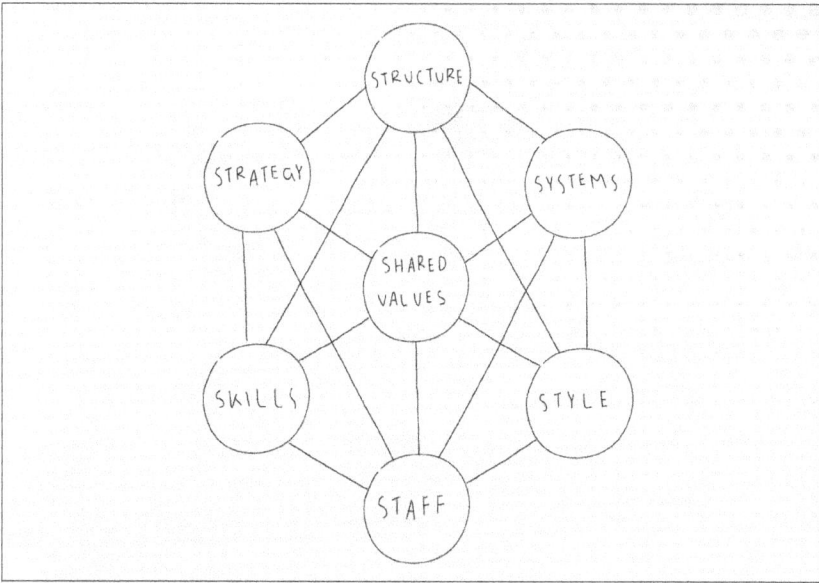

Figure 11-1: *The McKinsey & Co 7-S framework.*

Shared values

The centre of the McKinsey 7-S and our onboarding framework is shared values. All other aspects of the framework stem from what the organisation stands for, so it's crucial to **make sure your values and your employer's value overlap**. It's also vital to identify the behaviours that underpin these values *organisationally* and *personally*.

Structure

Like an iceberg, only a small part of an organisation's structures are visible, while the rest are hidden below the surface. You must **master both the formal, visible structures and the informal structures** within the organisation. Learning to adapt to the culture and prioritise relationships with the hidden network of Central Connectors and Information Brokers is also recommended. Remember - you are not an island.

Style

Your style is your personal brand, based on your unique skills, knowledge, experience, values and how you interact with others. You must learn to foster great initial impressions and **manage your personal brand** if you are to impress your new employer and fit in with those around you. The two most important aspects to display, in this regard, are warmth and competence.

Skills

In a work context, your skills are the distinctive capabilities that you have. When you learn to **apply your strengths to your role**, you not only achieve greater success but experience an increase in job satisfaction and meaning as well. Find your strengths and apply them, remembering to deal with any fears that show up for you as you do this.

Strategy

Although you may have clarity around your new role, it's critical to be able to articulate your employer's strategy and establish how to add value as well. The best way to do this is to get some quick wins under your belt by **setting up 1 or 2 winning projects**. Using your KPIs, CSFs, and LOS, choose projects that will help you climb up the learning and experience curves quickly, so you reach the point of competency fast.

Staff

Even when you understand an organisation's structures, you should be working to take this to the next level by learning to interact with those around you. The best way to do this is to gain a thorough understanding of **how to fit and where to contribute**. You will need to do your best to fit seamlessly into a team, follow their charter and be 110% responsible for your relationship with your manager.

Systems

When you commence your new role, you'll potentially face a variety of new systems. It's your job to get up to speed quickly and **learn how things work to support delivery**. Your best chance of doing this lies in accelerating your learning through the four stages of competence and by adopting a growth mindset.

UNDER REVIEW

The final step in your onboarding process, as discussed in Chapter 10, is your review. This is the time you can expect to be told how your manager views your performance, but it's more than that. You also have the opportunity to ask questions that will clarify your direction in your daily tasks, and even your future career within the organisation. Most of all, it's a chance to connect with your manager and prove your commitment. Remember to:

- Promote your successes
- Prepare considered responses
- Prepare questions that demonstrate your initiative
- Ask for a written record from your manager

This is the moment from when the rest of your career starts. I suggest you use this time wisely.

YOUR NEXT STEPS

1. Looking for another way to demonstrate your initiative?

Why not suggest that your new employer buys this book for their onboarding program to improve on their current hiring processes and make sure smoother transitions all around.

2. How did you go?

Please share how your career transition went beyond the first three months. I'd love to hear how this book helped you find your footing and navigate these precarious first few months. Email me at **gregw@wtfisnext.wtf**

3. Looking for additional resources?

Visit my **website wtfisnext.wtf**

And congratulations once again!

FOOTNOTES

Introduction

1   https://www.telegraph.co.uk/finance/jobs/10815017/
    Fifth-of-staff-on-probation-fail-trial-period-or-have-it-
    extended.html

2   https://www.shrm.org/resourcesandtools/hr-topics/
    employee-relations/pages/reducing-new-employee-
    turnover-among-emerging-adults.aspx

3   https://blog.clickboarding.com/18-jaw-dropping-
    onboarding-stats-you-need-to-know

4   https://blog.clickboarding.com/18-jaw-dropping-
    onboarding-stats-you-need-to-know

Chapter 1

1   https://medium.com/hr-blog-resources/top-6-
    employee-onboarding-statistics-2680704d3969

2   https://smith.queensu.ca/magazine/winter-2014/
    features/engaging-employees

3   http://www.hrmagazine.co.uk/article-details/a-fifth-of-
    employees-fail-to-pass-probation

4   https://hbr.org/2008/02/rapid-onboarding-at-capital-
    on.html

Chapter 2

1   https://hardwiredhumans.com/

2   https://docplayer.net/4194979-High-impact-leadership-
    transitions-a-transformative-approach.html

3   https://www2.deloitte.com/content/dam/Deloitte/
    global/Documents/About-Deloitte/gx-core-beliefs-
    and-culture.pdf

4   https://www.mckinsey.com/business-functions/
    strategy-and-corporate-finance/our-insights/
    enduring-ideas-the-7-s-framework

Chapter 3

1   https://www.linkedin.com/pulse/matching-personal-values-organizational-what-theory-ian-boreham/

2   https://www.stevepavlina.com/blog/2004/11/list-of-values/

3   https://www.researchgate.net/publication/268348803_The_Oxford_Handbook_of_Organizational_Psychology

Chapter4

1   https://www.organimi.com/reporting-relationships-structure-leads-way/

2   https://www.mckinsey.com/business-functions/organization/our-insights/harnessing-the-power-of-informal-employee-networks

3   https://www.mckinsey.com/business-functions/organization/our-insights/harnessing-the-power-of-informal-employee-networks

4   https://www.mckinsey.com/business-functions/organization/our-insights/harnessing-the-power-of-informal-employee-networks

5   https://www.mckinsey.com/featured-insights/leadership/company-philosophy-the-way-we-do-things-around-here

6   https://www.entrepreneur.com/article/270338

7   "FundamentalsofStrategy"byG.Johnson,R. Whittington,andK.Scholes.Publishedby Pearson Education, 2012.

8   https://www.mindtools.com/pages/article/newSTR_90.htm

9   "Corporate Cultures: The Rites and Rituals of Corporate Life." by T. Deal and A. 9. Kennedy. Published by Addison-Wesley Pub. Co, 1982.

10 https://www.google.com/url?q=https://hbr.
org/2002/06/the-people-who-make-organizations-go-
or-stop&sa=D&ust=1541716361876000&usg=AFQjCNHu
KCaxMxxxThFafG9k99etGrUKJA

11 https://www.mckinsey.com/business-functions/
organization/our-insights/the-role-of-networks-in-
organizational-change

12 https://www.mckinsey.com/business-functions/
organization/our-insights/the-role-of-networks-in-
organizational-change

13 https://www.mckinsey.com/business-functions/
organization/our-insights/the-role-of-networks-in-
organizational-change

Chapter 5

1 https://www.fastcompany.com/28905/brand-called-
you

2 http://www.psandman.com/col/reputation.htm

3 https://www.amazon.com/dp/1478930152/ref=as_
at?creativeASIN=1478930152&linkCode=w61&
imprToken=jUFVJze9RCJ79gE7X9pMDQ&slotNum=
0&tag=slatmaga-20

4 https://pdfs.semanticscholar.org/
df0c/9ca7be20ee0b7c5436332c20dcf46b2109d7.pdf

5 https://www.google.com/url?q=https://www.uwlax.edu/
urc/jur-online/PDF/2006/wiedmann.reinekin
g.pdf 5. &sa=D&ust= 5. 1543730006832000&usg=
5. AFQjCNE65oIdjb0g0h3XrzRoRWV0QxzpUw

6 https://journals.sagepub.com/doi/
abs/10.1177/1948550616662123

7 https://pdfs.semanticscholar.org/
a920/32341de4ca3d1551095c86506af7b54150f4.pdf

8 http://revisionisthistory.com/about

9 https://successwise.com/book/

Chapter 6

1   https://www.researchgate.net/profile/Paeivi_Vuokila-Oikkonen/post/Need_for_Resilience_articles/attachment/59d630fb79197b807798ec5a/AS%3A363732606701573%401463732019526/download/resilience_becker.pdf

2   https://www.zora.uzh.ch/id/eprint/63535/1/174_m_2012_HarzerRuch.pdf

3   http://www.viacharacter.org/blog/eight-reasons-why-you-should-talk-about-your-strengths/

4   https://news.gallup.com/opinion/gallup/196595/why-aren-organizations-strengths-based.aspx?g_source=CATEGORY_LEADERSHIP&g_medium=topic&g_campaign=tiles

5   https://www.researchgate.net/profile/Paeivi_Vuokila-Oikkonen/post/Need_for_Resilience_articles/attachment/59d630fb79197b807798ec5a/AS%3A363732606701573%401463732019526/download/resilience_becker.pdf

6   https://hbr.org/2005/01/how-to-play-to-your-strengths

7   https://hbr.org/2005/01/how-to-play-to-your-strengths

8   https://twitter.com/intent/tweet?url=http://mbuck.co/2nFn8q6&text=Most%20people%20are%20more%20fascinated%20by%20who%20they%20aren%27t%20and%20how%20to%20fix%20it%2C

9   %20instead%20of%20who%20they%20are%20and%20how%20to%20leverage%20it.%20&via=mwbuckingham&related=mwbuckingham

10 Marcus Buckingham and Donald Clifton, Now Discover YourStrengths

Chapter 7

1. https://thepalladiumgroup.com/research-impact/How-to-help-employees-understand-your-strategy
2. https://hbr.org/2008/04/can-you-say-what-your-strategy-is
3. https://hbr.org/2008/04/can-you-say-what-your-strategy-is
4. http://www.youngupstarts.com/2012/06/05/from-mailroom-to-boardroom-10-modern-day-execs-who-started-at-the-bottom/
5. https://www.hbs.edu/forum-for-growth-and-innovation/blog/post/Understanding-your-businesss-priorities
6. https://hbr.org/product/aligning-employees-through-line-of-sight/BH217-PDF-ENG
7. http://www.netmba.com/strategy/experience-curve/
8. https://www.referenceforbusiness.com/management/Em-Exp/Experience-and-Learning-Curves.html
9. https://www.danpink.com/books/when/
10. https://betterexplained.com/articles/understanding-the-pareto-principle-the-8020-rule/
11. https://www.mindtools.com/community/pages/article/newLDR_80.php
12. https://www.franklincovey.com/the-7-habits.html
13. https://www.mindtools.com/community/ExpertInterviews/KarenDillon.php
14. https://www.mindtools.com/community/ExpertInterviews/KarenDillon.php

Chapter 8

1   https://www.mindtools.com/community/pages/article/newLDR_86.php

2   https://project-management.com/the-five-stages-of-project-team-development/

3   https://hardwiredhumans.com/

4   https://project-management.com/the-five-stages-of-project-team-development/

5   https://www.mindtools.com/community/pages/article/newTMM_95.php

6   https://www.mindtools.com/community/pages/article/newHTE_87.php

7   https://www.mindtools.com/community/Bite-SizedTraining/SettingGoals.php

8   https://www.mindtools.com/community/Bite-SizedTraining/SettingGoals.php

9   https://www.cio.com.au/article/396365/leading_through_human_instincts/

10 https://www.mindtools.com/pages/article/Assertiveness.htm

11 https://www.mindtools.com/pages/article/Assertiveness.htm

Chapter 9

1 http://revisionisthistory.com/about

2 https://first20hours.com/

3 https://examinedexistence.com/the-four-states-of-competence-explained/

4 https://first20hours.com/

5 https://www.amazon.com/Mindset-Psychology-Carol-S-Dweck/dp/0345472322

6 https://www.mindtools.com/community/pages/article/mnemlsty.php

Chapter 10

1 https://www.cnbc.com/id/40840654

2 https://q12.gallup.com/public/en-us/Features

3 https://www.cnbc.com/id/40840654

4 https://www.cnbc.com/id/40840654

5 https://www.brighthr.com/articles/hiring/probation-periods/conducting-employee-probation-reviews

Conclusion

1 https://www.shrm.org/resourcesandtools/hr-topics/employee-relations/pages/reducing-new-employee-turnover-among-emerging-adults.aspx

2 https://blog.clickboarding.com/18-jaw-dropping-onboarding-stats-you-need-to-know

INDEX

INDEX

INDEX

INDEX

S

www.ingramcontent.com/pod-product-compliance
Lightning Source LLC
Chambersburg PA
CBHW071338210326
41597CB00015B/1488